The Hixon Railway Disaster

To, Howard, and Pip, best wishes,

Richard Westwood

The Hixon Railway Disaster

The Inside Story

Richard Westwood

PEN & SWORD
TRANSPORT

First published in Great Britain in 2017 by
Pen & Sword Transport
An imprint of Pen & Sword Books Ltd
Pen & Sword Books Ltd
47 Church Street
Barnsley
South Yorkshire
S70 2AS

ISBN 9781473884434

Printed and bound by CPI Group (UK) Ltd, Croydon, CR0 4YY

Pen & Sword Books Ltd incorporates the Imprints of Pen & Sword
Archaeology, Atlas, Aviation, Battleground, Discovery, Family History,
History, Maritime, Military, Naval, Politics, Railways, Select, Transport,
True Crime, Fiction, Frontline Books, Leo Cooper, Praetorian Press,
Seaforth Publishing, Wharncliffe and White Owl.

For a complete list of Pen & Sword titles please contact
PEN & SWORD BOOKS LIMITED
47 Church Street, Barnsley, South Yorkshire, S70 2AS, England
E-mail: enquiries@pen-and-sword.co.uk
Website: www.pen-and-sword.co.uk

To the memory of John Hilton
killed, together with four members of his family
16 April 1968
R. I. P.

Contents

Preface   The Leominster connection   ix

Chapter 1   'You can't park that there, mate!'   1

Chapter 2   The legal stuff and the Men from The Ministry   20

Chapter 3   Murphy's Law, or the Engineer's Touchstone   28

Chapter 4   'Well the lorry driver and his mate took off in
high dudgeon, and we went home'   47

Chapter 5   The Chopping Block   56

Chapter 6   The Hixon Inquiry gets under way and the
Railway Inspectorate has a nasty shock   63

Chapter 7   Tragedy at Trent Road level-crossing, Beckingham,
Lincolnshire: Tuesday, 16 April 1968   85

Chapter 8   The mind of a Judge (and the cost of copper wire)   90

Chapter 9   Tommy Cromwell: Tuesday, 5 December 1967   104

Chapter 10   The dogs that didn't bark   107

Afterword   Precursor: Leominster, Kington junction
level-crossing, 4 May 1965   110

Postscript   112

Acknowledgements and Sources   113

Index   117

The Leominster connection

*What happened at Leominster, Kington junction level-crossing,
on 8 November 1966, and how and why an inconvenient truth
was covered up*

T his book came to be written largely because having taken early retirement
from my job as a teacher, due to ill health, and finding myself with time
on my hands, I decided to investigate an alarming incident that took
place at a railway level-crossing at Leominster in Herefordshire in 1966, which
I knew my father had been involved with. Initially I thought it would probably
provide enough material for an article for one of the many railway heritage
magazines. However, it soon became clear that 'the more I looked, the more
I found' and in order to do both my father and the story justice, a short book
was required; mainly because what happened at Leominster merely pointed the
way to a startling re-assessment of both the dreadful accident that occurred at
Hixon level-crossing in Staffordshire early in 1968, and more particularly the
subsequent Public Court of Inquiry and its findings.

I am of the first generation from both sides of my family, for approximately
150 years, not to have worked on the railways. Indeed, one of my early memories
is of using a little contraption to roll my grandfather some cigarettes to take on
shift with him; he was a foreman shunter at what, prior to 1964, was the station,
goods yards and junction at Leominster. The junction, Kington junction, as
it was known, was just under half a mile to the north of the station, with a
single-line branch heading off to the west, towards Kington and Presteigne.
When the final train ran over the branch on 24 September 1964, it was my
grandfather, Bert Pemberton, as the longest serving railwayman working on
the branch who was given the honour of being the guard on it. Within six
months he had retired, the goods yards were moth-balled prior to closure, and
the branch-line track had been taken up and its points removed. By May 1965,
Kington junction, which had existed for well over a century, was no more. What
was left behind was a level-crossing and a redundant signal-box, although the
signalman, whilst having no signal levers to pull, still had the important task of
opening and closing the crossing gates.

But not for very much longer, because following Dr Richard Beeching's 'reforms', in common with quite a few other level-crossings across the country, Leominster's was now seen as being ideal for conversion to fully automatic working. On the face of things the new situation was compelling, in particular there were the excellent views of the crossing at Leominster for approaching train drivers, for many hundreds of yards in both directions along the Up and the Down railway lines and in particular on the (unusually) southbound Down line, where in daylight the crossing was visible from nearly a mile away.

Some of the express passenger trains on the Welsh Marches line, those on the Cardiff to Holyhead service, were not scheduled to stop at Leominster station, and whereas previously the existence of the branch-line junction, goods yards and their associated workings, might have inhibited a good proportion of these trains from operating at maximum speed over the level-crossing and through the station, now there were no such inhibitions. In fact, once the crossing had been converted to automatic working, train drivers were instructed to travel at 90 miles per hour in order to better facilitate the timely operation of the newly installed half-barrier crossing. As well as, of course, helping to reduce the average journey time.

George Orwell, who is not a bad role model for any author, gave as one of his primary reasons for writing that 'there is some lie I want to expose, some fact to which I want to draw attention, and my initial concern is to get a hearing'. This quotation sums up, rather well, what lies behind my five-year-long, self-imposed task of getting to the bottom of what went on, and what went wrong, with the inquiry into an infamous railway accident that took place almost half a century ago. In point of fact, two accidents, and two inquiries, because as well as the collision at Hixon level-crossing, in Staffordshire, in January 1968, there was also the ghastly tragedy at Trent Road level-crossing, at Beckingham in Lincolnshire, in April 1968.

It has become increasingly clear to me that on the balance of probabilities, both of these accidents would not have occurred if one man, Colonel W. P. Reed, of the Railway Inspectorate, had taken the appropriate and necessary action, upon having received in good time, a report of what had happened at Leominster level-crossing, on 8 November 1966, nearly fourteen months prior to the Hixon collision. I will leave it to the reader to decide what lies, if any, have been exposed, although the facts, as I have disinterred them and laid them out, should certainly speak for themselves. As to who will 'get a hearing', it is my sincere hope that two groups whose voices went largely unheeded and whose views were often disregarded during the Hixon Inquiry, will get some small recognition at last for coping so well, with the novel and potentially lethal devices that had been put amongst them in such a cavalier and inept manner: first, the ordinary vehicle-driving public of this country (including policemen and heavy haulage drivers) and finally, the 'poor bloody railwaymen'.

Orwell also makes a good point about his being primarily motivated to write in order to put the record straight, 'to find out true facts and store them up for the use of posterity'. I would certainly share this basic motivation in relation to the subject matter of this book; in particular because I believe I have demonstrated that senior members of the Railway Inspectorate together with senior officials of the Ministry of Transport knowingly and deliberately concealed 'true facts' from the Hixon Inquiry, and by so doing escaped receiving their just deserts: the full culpability for constructing the circumstances of the Hixon collision and that culpability's consequent likely repercussions, which again, on the balance of probabilities, would have included at least one Manslaughter indictment on the grounds of gross negligence.

Specifically, judging by the documentary evidence, as well as Colonel Reed, Colonel Denis McMullen, the Chief Inspecting Officer of Railways, together with Mr C. P. Scott-Malden, the Under-Secretary for the Railways Group of the Ministry of Transport, at the time, were both well aware of a lengthy history of disturbing incidents involving near collisions between road vehicles and trains at one level-crossing in particular – Leominster, Kington junction – which were of direct relevance to the Hixon Inquiry; and that they failed to reveal any of this knowledge to the Chairman of the Hixon Inquiry, largely because the adversarial structure and strict evidence testing procedures and protocols of that inquiry, gave them the opportunity to keep things to themselves. Oh, and of course, the motivation to do just that.

Trying to write an accurate account of events that happened nearly half a century ago, can leave one feeling a bit like poor old Sir Walter Raleigh, who having himself seen the apparent murder of a workman from the window of his prison cell in the Tower of London, was subsequently unable, despite making diligent enquiries, to establish to his satisfaction the truth of what had occurred. Having been foiled in describing and understanding something that had happened under his nose as it were, Raleigh then abandoned his partly completed 'History of the World' on the grounds that he could not be sure of the veracity of any of it. Fortunately, the events described in the present book nearly all generated a considerable written record, whether in official documents or in the news media of the time. So the process became one of sifting the reliable information from the unreliable.

It was useful not to have to argue out the strength and admissibility of each piece of evidence in open court, as had occurred with the Hixon Inquiry itself, but rather to be able to employ something similar to the inquisitorial techniques, and the more informal ways of proceeding, of the Railway Inspectorate's tried and tested investigative methodology, which can be summarized as: establish the causation and chronology of events pertaining to an accident or serious incident, then apportion the blame (and occasionally, to be fair, the approbation) and finally, suggest a remedy. In short, to 'follow the evidence'. Using this approach, and having access to the archived documents of not only the Hixon Inquiry but also the Ministry of Transport, together with a wide range of newspaper and other media files, I have been able to 'follow the evidence'. Of course, those in charge of the Hixon Inquiry would not have been able to access the Ministry of Transport records directly in 1968; instead they had to rely upon the statements of the Ministry witnesses and those supporting documents the Ministry was requested to put in front of the Inquiry. Putting it simply, because the inquiry 'did not know what it did not know', it therefore did not ask for, or receive, the specific documentary evidence that would have established clear and direct lines of accountability for decisions taken. The Railway Inspectorate on the other hand, nearly always began their accident or serious incident investigations having a very good idea of what they didn't know, and usually moved rapidly forward by asking questions directly, of those who they knew were in a position to give, and moreover, obliged (being railway employees) to provide accurate answers.

The great irony of the Hixon Inquiry's very wide spreading of responsibility for the collision at Hixon level-crossing ('Rockets all round in the Hixon Report' as the trade paper *Commercial Motor* put it at the time) is that if that Inquiry had itself been conducted after the manner of an accident or serious incident investigation by the Railway Inspectorate, then virtually the entire responsibility for the Hixon collision, and the associated botched introduction of automatic railway level-crossings into this country, would quite quickly, and quite correctly, have been laid at the door of … the Railway Inspectorate.

Richard Westwood
Clevedon, North Somerset
April 2017

Chapter 1

'You can't park that there, mate!'

What follows primarily concerns the actions of two men, who may never even have spoken to each other and yet who had a considerable influence on each other's lives, albeit in very different ways. One of them was my father, Reuben John (Jack) Westwood, and the other was Colonel William Power (W. P.) Reed, of the Railway Inspectorate, which at that time comprised an important, indeed the dominant, section of the Railways Group of the Ministry of Transport. (For ease of reading, whenever the 'Railway Inspectorate' or 'Inspectorate' is referred to in the text this also means 'the Railways Group of the Ministry of Transport'; the two were to all intents and purposes synonymous as far as the oversight of the installation of automatic, train-initiated level-crossings was concerned.)

The Railway Inspectorate's main role was, of course, the maintenance and regulation of the high standards of safety enjoyed by Britain's Railways, through the investigation of railway accidents and serious incidents notified to them by the operators of the railways. However, in the mid-1950s the British Transport Commission extended the Inspectorate's remit by charging them with supervising the modernization of railway level-crossing arrangements in this country; the logic being that as the acknowledged guardians of railway safety, who better than the Inspectorate to oversee the transition from one safe, but 'creaking', system of level-crossing protection to a modern, efficient, but equally safe system.

In the early years of the installation process progress was very slow, and most of the small number of new crossings that were installed, went into quiet locations on the Eastern Region of British Railways. It was not until a policy decision was taken in 1963 to automate crossings with relatively high road-vehicle usage, and relatively high numbers of trains travelling at high speed, that significant numbers of conversions took place over the rail network as a whole. A lot of the credit for the increase in the rate and number of installations, must undoubtedly go to Colonel Reed who, from November 1961 until January 1968, was in operational charge of the introduction of automatic, train-initiated level-crossings into this country. However, the actual physical installation of the new equipment was the responsibility of each one of the six separate geographical regions of British Railways. As Colonel Reed made clear in a model opening speech he prepared in

November 1965, for the use of presiding officers, at the initial site meetings that were held prior to every proposed conversion to automatic working:

> Let me introduce myself. I am an Inspecting Officer of Railways, with special responsibilities in regard to changes of methods of operating level-crossings ... The Railway are responsible at law for providing and maintaining protection at level-crossings ... [the Railway Inspectorate] exercise jurisdiction and is responsible for standards of safety – not by inspection of maintenance: that is the Railway's duty – but by approval of new installations.

It is worth emphasizing, at this early stage, this supposed distinction between the roles of British Railways and the Railway Inspectorate: both roles are rooted in the very similar legal duties of care that each held towards, not just the users of the railway, but the public in general. Any such distinction is at best a fine one, and certainly not one that would have been thought important by anyone outside the railway industry, as far as ensuring the provision of fit-for-purpose level-crossings was concerned. By drawing attention to it early on in his model speech, Colonel Reed may have been seeking to reassure those attending the initial site meetings that the conversions to automatic working were being done under strict and impartial supervision. Attendance at initial site meetings was by invitation only and limited to what British Railways considered to be interested parties: typically, representatives of the police, the local authority where the crossing was located, the local authority responsible for highway maintenance, the Roads Engineering Division of the Ministry of Transport, and if the crossing was in a rural area, the National Farmers' Union (NFU). These initial site meetings were essentially 'for the convenience of the railway', and what is more the attendees were not really required to give their opinions, but rather were primarily there to be informed of what British Railways was going to bring about. Moreover, these meetings were the only occasion that was scheduled into the conversion process, where legitimate interest groups from outside the railway industry, or Ministry of Transport, were invited to make *any contribution at all*; and this consultation generally took place a year or more before work began on automating the individual level-crossing in question.

It is apparent from a perusal of the model speech, which would have taken around twenty minutes to deliver in full, that Colonel Reed wanted the new automatic crossings presented primarily, as a means of 'saving attendance' and therefore making a huge financial gain nationally (the equivalent of over a billion pounds annually in today's money). The saving of waiting time at crossings for the motorist is the secondary reason put forward in favour and thirdly – stated almost as an afterthought – the potential 'to increase railway operating efficiency [because] ... the protecting signals at public level-crossings are not correctly spaced for modern multiple aspect signalling and if they can be done away with the capacity of the line is much improved'. This last benefit of automation was expressed in technical jargon, which was probably deliberately intended to go right over the heads of most non-railwaymen present. It highlighted the removal of interlocking signal protection at level-crossings, and it was this, of course, which made the whole automation project worthwhile for the railway industry, 'the icing on the cake' as it were.

Specifically, the effect of much improving line capacity led directly to significantly improving performance in the single area where rail already had a clear advantage over road transport (and the nascent internal airlines) and that was moving passengers quickly and efficiently from city centre to city centre. In order to increase the average speed of express trains, they needed to be able to operate at close to their maximum speed for longer periods of time. The new train-initiated, automated crossings would deliver this optimized maximum by cutting out the need for any diminution of speed, except where the train was slowed to a stop at a station. Colonel Reed was responsible for specifying to train drivers that speeds were to be kept as close to maximum as possible, and that they were not to slow down when approaching the new crossings. He was clearly anxious that the Railway exploited to the full this new advantage of 'increased capacity' given to it by automation of the crossings. In fact, this single consideration seems to have become dominant in Colonel Reed's attitude towards the automation process, of which, let it not be forgotten, he was in day-to-day charge. He sought to protect this increased capacity to the extent that he did his best to reduce to a bare minimum the actual physical means by which the newly speeded-up trains could be made to slow down, or stop. Putting it bluntly he wanted as few telephones, for the use of the public, installed in the barrier mechanisms of the new crossings as possible, because he thought that they might be misused by pranksters and cause unnecessary delays for trains. In the light of subsequent events, this reasoning is hard to accept at face value (and was so for many at the time).

Colonel Reed considered that the likelihood of vehicles stalling and getting stuck on level-crossings with a train imminent was remote, and therefore, was an acceptable risk *because* it was so remote. As he saw things, the whole point of having the trains trigger the crossing mechanisms, was that they would arrive on the crossings very rapidly; indeed the new system was deliberately designed for the trains to be too close to be stopped. So literally, there was no point in having telephones in the barriers. Colonel Reed seems to have believed that there were likely to be very few, if any, *legitimate* reasons why anyone would need to make an emergency call from one of the automatic crossings. Having said that, he was aware that there was some anxiety about the safety of the new crossings, which he did attempt to address in his model speech through reassurances, such as: 'The automatic crossing ... can also obviate certain causes of accident particularly those due to a mistake by a crossing keeper ... though it should not be thought that the manned crossing is dangerous and the automatic barrier utterly safe.' Altogether then, the model speech sets out a cogent and well-argued case in favour of the automation of level-crossings. However, what is extremely perturbing is that although there is a reference to 'additional safeguards which can be provided at awkward sites', there is no mention whatsoever in this lengthy document of the provision of telephones for the use of the public in the event of an emergency. Nor even telephones for the use of two particular sub-sets of the public in routine non-emergency situations, specifically farmers herding animals across crossings, and secondly vehicle drivers with abnormal loads. It should be stressed that historical hindsight is not being deployed here, because Colonel Reed had been personally responsible in 1964, for approving the wording and design of a pair of identical signboards (one for each road carriageway) to be used at all automatic crossings where telephones for the use of the public were being provided. These signboards were supposed to alert members of the public to the existence of telephones and the circumstances when they needed to be used. Because he had such an intimate and detailed knowledge of, and kept such a tight grip on, every aspect of the level-crossing automation project, it is inconceivable that Colonel Reed would merely have forgotten to mention that there was a need at some crossings for telephones for the use of the public. Precisely and paradoxically, because he was of the opinion that most crossings should not have such telephones.

Therefore, the key to understanding why there is no mention of telephones in the model speech, is that the enabling legislation for level-crossing automation, that back in 1959 had specified telephones for the use of the public built into the barriers of every installation, had been changed at the behest of Colonel Reed. From 1963 onwards the 'default model' for automatic level-crossing installations had no telephones for the use of the public. This raises and answers a seemingly trivial question but one which is actually of overwhelming importance as far as the Hixon accident was concerned; there was no mention of telephones in the November 1965 model speech, because Colonel Reed did not want there to be any public telephones in most of the subsequent installations. Quite simply, he sought to avoid raising the possibility with attendees at the individual initial site meetings up and down the country, in order to keep the number of crossings with telephones as low as possible. In those few locations where telephones were to be fitted, Reed envisaged these being in rural areas where the reasons for obtaining clearance prior to venturing onto the railway were either permission to take across a herd of animals, or to manoeuvre across an abnormal agricultural vehicle such as a combine harvester. Here, he considered his cleverly designed signboard would be sufficient to provide notice to the small number of people who would need it. The evidence for believing that Colonel Reed had this negative attitude towards telephones for the use of the public, is not just limited to his model speech, because there exist minutes of an initial site meeting from May 1965. In these minutes, he argues the point (if not quite the toss!) with an NFU representative, that telephones were not necessary at that particular location: this was at Leominster, Kington junction.

Now, although Colonel Reed considered that he was in overall charge of Automatic Half Barrier (AHB) crossing installation and that therefore British Railways were obliged to fit the crossings according to his instructions, understandably perhaps, there seems to have been something of a reluctance on the part of British Railways to install crossings without telephones for the use of the public. In the case of Leominster for instance (and happily for all concerned, as we shall see), although there were no telephones built into the barrier housings, there was a single phone provided, mounted in a small metal cabinet on the warning lights mast on the Ludlow side of the crossing. This phone was for the use of farmers wishing to herd animals over the crossing. The situation across the country, from 1963 when the legislation was introduced specifying no barrier telephones as the default position, through to October of 1966, seems to have been that British Railways did their best to provide at least some form of permanent telephone for the use of the public at the newly converted crossings. Moreover, at some crossings up and down the country, the previous equipment used to communicate between the old manned crossing and its covering signal-box was left in place. (This was the case at Hixon AHB crossing, where there were both two newly installed barrier phones and a pre-conversion handset mounted in a small crossing keeper's shelter adjacent to the Up line. The original specification for Hixon made in early 1966, was to have had no telephones for the use of the public in the barriers. It is worth pointing out that the only call made from Hixon AHB crossing prior to the disaster, concerning an exceptional or heavy load, was made by an escorting policeman on behalf of a Wynns' driver, Mr T. C. (Tommy) Cromwell, on Thursday, 7 December 1967. That call was to check if there was sufficient clearance under the 25 kilovolt catenary wiring, not to see if it was safe to cross; the call was made from the old pre-conversion handset, not one of the barrier phones that were later criticized in the report for being very hard to locate.)

So, one way or another, only eighteen automatic crossings out of approximately 200 across the UK were without telephones by January 1968. Colonel Reed had obviously been aware of this tendency on the part of British Railways to provide telephones against the thrust of his 1963 Requirements; his response was to reiterate the instructions for 'no telephones' in fresh legislation of July 1966. However, this must have been the final straw for British Railways, because a decision was taken by the Chief Telecommunications and Signals Engineer, Mr John Tyler, to provide telephones for the use of the public, in all barrier mechanisms authorized from October 1966, directly contradicting Colonel Reed's wishes. Crucially, this decision was taken at a national level by

British Railways, thus giving no opportunity for the six individual regional managements to be 'picked off' by Colonel Reed, or any other member of the Railway Inspectorate. The six regions were Eastern, London Midland, North Eastern, Scotland, Southern, and Western; and the relationship between their senior managements and the Inspectorate, was heavily influenced by the unequal power gradient, inherent in the primary safety and regulatory role of the Inspectorate. Putting it bluntly, when Colonel Reed and his colleagues said 'Jump' the expectation that had grown up since the nationalization of the Railways in 1948 was that the response from British Railways management would be, 'How high, sir?' Therefore, it is no surprise that the same expectation was in place, as far the Inspectorate's additional responsibility of overseeing the introduction of automated crossings was concerned. Also, whilst Colonel Reed was in day-to-day charge of the conversion process, it had become the pet project of the whole Railway Inspectorate, together with the senior civil servants of the Railways Group of the Ministry of Transport; Colonel McMullen as the Chief Inspecting Officer and Mr Scott-Malden, the Under-Secretary for the Railways Group, could always be relied upon to 'lean' upon any recalcitrant British Railways regional manager. (As will become clear from their interaction with Mr Lattimer, Assistant General Manager of Western Region, concerning the hair-raising 'Colonel Gower' incident at Leominster level-crossing early in December 1966.)

It is important to realize that evidence of this strange and dangerous 'turf war' over telephone provision would not have been instantly apparent to those in charge of the Hixon Inquiry, but plenty of people in senior positions knew what had been happening; particularly, of course, Colonel Reed, who was never really asked to explain why he reversed the earlier policy of providing telephones in all of the crossing barriers, to one where the norm was to have none. Indeed, the deliberately misleading account, that the crossings without telephones were those which had been installed early on in the conversion process, was allowed to become the accepted reality during the Hixon Inquiry.

Anyway, the stage was set for some dramatic events at Leominster crossing and fortunately – no thanks to Colonel Reed – there was a telephone, of sorts, available for instant use. Also the signals protecting Leominster station track section, which were co-incidentally able to offer protection for the level-crossing as well, had not yet been 'done away with'. That too proved to be fortunate. Colonel Reed was obviously an intelligent, knowledgeable and dedicated man, he knew his job and had great confidence in the superiority of the new level-crossing arrangements he was overseeing. However, it is instructive to be able to judge from his model speech, as to where he regarded the legal limits of the Railway Inspectorate's – that is, *his* – responsibility for automatic crossings to lie, he was just there to approve installations, apparently. Although, as will become clear, in reality he paid no more than lip-service to the idea that British

Railways should be allowed to produce, install and operate the new equipment without being closely supervised as to every detail. The astonishing reason he wished to have control over virtually every aspect of AHB crossing installation was that he and his two senior colleagues, Colonel McMullen and Under-Secretary Scott-Malden, were deeply committed to what they referred to as the AHB 'cause', because they believed that it held the key to the provision of rapid and relatively cheap inter-city express rail travel. Incredibly, Leominster level-crossing, far from being typical and unremarkable in comparison to other AHB crossings, was singled out for special consideration by Reed, McMullen and Scott-Malden; effectively it was being used as the key part of a 'test-bed' project to see how much the running capacity of the Welsh Marches main line could be increased, and of course this was being done under conditions of appropriate secrecy. (Initially, the Beeching proposals for the Welsh Marches line published in 1963, had been to close most of the stations, except for Newport, Shrewsbury and Chester and furthermore all the stations between Chester and Holyhead were to close. Then, express passenger trains hauled by the superb new Class 37 diesel locomotives would be able to run at high speed for long distances, untrammelled by the need to slow down (or heaven forbid, stop) because all of the old fully gated level-crossings interlocked with signals would have been replaced with AHBs. The in-coming Labour Government of 1964 had rejected this radical plan to provide a high-speed rail link from one end of Wales to the other, but that didn't stop its proponents in the Inspectorate from persevering with increasing line capacity for selected parts of the Welsh Marches line, such as that between Shrewsbury and Hereford.)

My father, Jack Westwood, also worked on Britain's railways: he was an assistant linesman (or assistant signals and telecommunication technician, as they were later designated). Together with his three workmates he maintained and repaired railway signals, telephones, and other equipment between Hereford and Shrewsbury. He retired from the job he loved in April 1987, and received a lump sum of £2,999.26, as part of his pension settlement, together with a separate cheque for exactly £4,000. At first he could not figure out what this latter amount was for, as there was no explanation given, just the cheque with a cursory payment slip labelled, 'Ex gratia, British Railways' Board' ... then he recalled what had occurred some twenty-one years previously in the winter of 1966.

He and his workmates had recently converted the level-crossing, on the northern outskirts of the small town of Leominster in Herefordshire, to AHB status. The mechanical and electrical installations were fully completed; it was functioning as an automatic crossing, and had been for some weeks. The crossing's location was, and still is, on the main Welsh Marches railway line, where, in 1966, it intersected with the A49, a busy trunk road, at that time carrying a large amount of heavy traffic between the industrial North of England and South Wales.

According to my father, on this particular day it was getting close to 'knocking off time, and was dropping down dark' when he saw a Scammell articulated low-loader, with a mobile crane on board, grounded on the crossing. The Scammell rig had come from the direction of Ludlow, heading south, the driver's cab was clear of the tracks on the Leominster side of the crossing; however, the trailer was stuck, with its considerable load positioned squarely between the two railway lines, the jib of the crane stretching back behind it to the Ludlow side. The low-loader was obviously a deadly hazard, stationary as it was. Without pausing to explain what he was doing, to his workmates or the supervising Signals and Telecommunication Inspector, my father ran across to the other side of the crossing, to a phone mounted on a warning lights mast positioned close to the railway tracks and intended for local farmers to contact the monitoring signal-box, to check that it was safe to move animals over the crossing. My father knew that a passenger express, comprising eight carriages at the least, and hauled by a large Class 37 diesel locomotive, was due very soon, next scheduled stop Hereford. It would be approaching Leominster crossing at the officially prescribed operating speed of 90 miles per hour and the only hope of halting the train, or at this late stage slowing it down, was to warn the signalman in the Leominster South End signal-box (which was located nearly a mile away) to put the two signals, Distant and Home, protecting the Leominster station track section, to 'danger'. As he was making the call, the bells began to ring, the warning lights to flash, and the barriers came down. This meant that the oncoming train had already passed the Distant signal, positioned some 900 yards north of the level-crossing; however, the signalman was able to switch the Home signal (which as its name implies was much closer to the crossing, located only 300 yards away) in time for the train driver to see it and to apply the brakes. This then gave the train approximately 600 yards for it to slow down in, as the brakes took effect, and crucially, of course, before it reached the level-crossing.

Meanwhile, on the other side of the tracks, events seem to have played out as follows: one of the railwaymen present, probably humorously, à la William 'Mate' Cobblers of *The Goon Show*, shouted to the lorry driver, 'You can't park that there, mate!' The driver informed the railwaymen, in no uncertain terms, that his trailer was well and truly stuck and that they must get on the phone and stop the trains, whilst he jacked it up, to get it off the crossing. He was told that there was a train due imminently and that it was far too late to stop it. The four railwaymen on the Leominster side of the crossing, together with the lorry driver's assistant, then withdrew to a safe distance, expecting a catastrophe to unfold, which they knew they would have had to cope with. The driver, heroically (and fortunately) disregarded the advice to abandon his stranded lorry and instead got back into the cab, intending to jerk-start the engine of his tractor unit and thereby to drag the trailer clear.

Which is what he did, with the express train running onto the crossing behind him, and missing the rear of the rig by mere inches, just as the trailing crane jib cleared the southbound Down line.

In the April of 1987, looking back from a distance in time of over twenty years, my father could remember several things relating to his part in preventing a collision: firstly, upon his return to the Leominster side of the level crossing, the supervising Signals and Telecommunication (S&T) Inspector, a young man named Hallett, wondered where he had gone, and initially, until he was disabused, presumed he had merely run off to get out of harm's way. Secondly, my father recalled that he was summoned to Reading for an inquiry, *at some point*, around that time, to give his account of the incident. The chairman of this investigating panel, apparently a former officer of the Royal Engineers, stated unequivocally, that only the simultaneous but independent actions of both the lorry driver and my father had averted a disaster, neither one alone would have been sufficient. This ex-officer also asked about what my father had done during the Second World War, possibly expecting him to have been in the armed forces. Presumably, it would have been this panel which recommended an ex-gratia sum of £5,000 for my father. The thing which initially intrigued me was, why was the bulk of this payment, £4,000, delayed until 1987?

The answer to this question, as I have discovered, lay in the extensive documentation relating to the dreadful collision at another automatic level-crossing, at Hixon in Staffordshire, which took place on Saturday, 6 January 1968, nearly fourteen months after the near-miss at Leominster. What occurred at Hixon was so appalling that it sent shock-waves, not just through the railway industry, but throughout British society as a whole. On a clear winter's day, at around 12.26 p.m., a Manchester to Euston express on the recently electrified West Coast Main Line, ran into a huge heavy-haulage rig, 148 feet long and weighing over 160 tons, which was crawling at just two miles per hour over an automatic level-crossing, installed some ten months previously, in April 1967. According to witnesses on board, the train was slowing from its locally restricted speed of 85 mph and was probably travelling at 75 mph at the moment of impact. The locomotive's two-man crew would first have seen the blocked level-crossing at a distance of approximately 300 yards, as they rounded a curve on the line, which then gave just nine seconds for an emergency brake application to take effect.

Eleven people lost their lives in the Hixon collision, with many more being seriously injured. The question for the railway industry and the Government, that had to be answered and urgently, was: how could this have happened? The West Coast Main Line was, after all, British Railways' flagship project, its refurbishment still only partially completed by 1968; a huge investment was being made electrifying and modernizing the line between Euston and Glasgow, so that it was the equal of any railway in the world, not just the twenty-five kilovolt alternating current catenary system that provided the power for the locomotives, but the state-of-the-art signalling system, and, of course, several train-activated automatic level-crossings, which were not linked in, in any way, to the signalling system, as far as normal activation of the crossing barriers was concerned (although the automatic system could be overridden, and the barriers then controlled by railway personnel, directly, if it was thought necessary to do so).

Just how totemic the West Coast Main Line was, not just to British Railways but also to the Labour Government of the time, can be judged by a speech made by the Minister of Transport, Barbara Castle, to her Party's Conference in 1966: 'What does this electrification scheme really mean for Britain? Obviously it's going to be a showpiece, not only, I hope of the Railways, but also a showpiece of what we mean when we talk about the Modernization of Britain. This is Modernization.' The incoming Labour Government of 1964, whilst accepting and implementing most of the Beeching Plan's recommendations (which had been drawn up under the previous Conservative Government) had overruled Beeching's objections to further electrification of the West Coast Main Line, and by April 1966 there was a full regular service between London and Manchester, with a journey time of just two and a half hours. Now, with this, the 'Jewel in the Crown' of the Government's modernization plans apparently in serious trouble, Barbara Castle, convened a Judge-led Public Court of Inquiry to investigate, not just what had gone so tragically wrong at Hixon, but to assess and report upon the entire programme of the installation of automatic level-crossings across the rail network as a whole.

This was the first such public inquiry into a railway accident since the Tay Bridge Disaster Inquiry of 1880, because although, obviously, there had been many railway accidents between the two, these had all been investigated by the Railway Inspectorate, a small, elite group of civil servants, made up exclusively, since its foundation in 1840, of former officers of the Royal Engineers. There were five Railway Inspecting Officers in early 1968, in order of seniority: Colonel Denis McMullen (the Chief Inspecting Officer), Colonel W. P. Reed, Colonel J. R. H. Robertson, Lieutenant-Colonel I. K. A. McNaughton and Major Peter Olver.

Three of the Inspectorate, McMullen, Reed and Olver were closely involved in overseeing the introduction of automatic crossings; as the Chief Inspecting Officer, Colonel McMullen's primary role was to definitively sign off each individual AHB crossing conversion, having received all the documentation for each crossing, including, of course, the final site meeting report. Whereas Reed and Olver were, firstly, kept very busy liaising with each of British Railways' six constituent regions as to their proposals for level-crossing automation, then presiding over the initial site meetings, then reviewing British Railways' detailed plans for each conversion and finally holding a commissioning site meeting after the event, sometimes as much as three months or more after the change to automation had taken place.

Secondly, there was advice to be given at a national level, over rules and regulations concerning how all the AHB crossings were to be operated by the Railway, including for example, decisive input as to what messages should be on the various signs considered necessary to alert the general public as to how they ought to behave when confronted by one of the new crossings. On top of all this an eye had to be kept on any perceived problems there might be with the new equipment. Although, of course, the Railway Inspectorate relied upon the railway authorities reporting any accidents, or serious incidents that happened on the rail network to them, or rather to the Railways Group of the Ministry of Transport, of which they were a part. Altogether then, a considerable and expanding area of responsibility for the Railway Inspectorate; indeed this burgeoning workload had been recognized, to some degree at least, because Major Olver had been recruited in 1965 to work alongside Colonel Reed, exclusively on the AHB crossing programme. As is pointed out in paragraph 57 of the *Hixon Inquiry Report*, nobody ever really took an overview of exactly how this programme should be managed, instead, like Topsy, it just grew.

There was also another aspect to the control that the Railway Inspectorate exercised over automatic crossing installation, that it was only *partial* control, in particular as far as two seemingly peripheral aspects of the installations were concerned: firstly, the publicity aimed at the vehicle-driving public to inform them of the existence of the new crossings, and secondly the provision and placement of signage at the AHB crossings themselves. As to publicity, although Colonel Reed made a good case, from 1963 onwards, for an appropriate national information campaign to accompany the automation programme, this was not taken up by the Ministry of Transport's publicity department, who had the final say-so. Regarding the specifications for the warning signage, there is clear evidence that Colonel Reed was directly responsible for both the wording and 'dual-purpose' design of the

IN EMERGENCY
or before crossing
with exceptional or
heavy loads or cattle
PHONE SIGNALMAN

signboard that was to be placed at those AHB crossings which had been provided with phones for the use of the public. The signboards were produced by British Railway's own engineering department, so although Reed had a direct advisory role as far as the design was concerned, the actual placement, and crucially, the orientation of these signs in relation to the carriageway by the railway technicians erecting the new crossings, was subject to yet more advice from a different part of the Ministry of Transport, that is the Road Group, Engineering Department.

As becomes increasingly apparent, this combination of uncertainty with the actual purpose of the signboard, added to more uncertainty as to which way it should face in relation to the road carriageway is, in the opinion of the author of this book, the single most important causal factor leading to the collision at Hixon level-crossing. Whilst the *Hixon Inquiry Report* does give great prominence to problems with this particular signboard, it does not identify it as the primary causal factor. My assertion is simply, that if the Hixon Inquiry had properly pursued the evidence trails in existence at the time, in the files of the Ministry of Transport and British Railways, then the intervention made by Colonel Reed in April 1964 when he 'suggested' the full text and layout of the signboard, would have been seen as the essential causal element in the chain of events leading to the Hixon collision. Without his obsessive and unfortunate overlooking, it is at least possible that the British Railways S&T Department, left to get on with the job by themselves would have come up with the two separate signs, correctly placed in two locations and differently oriented that were necessary for the two distinct messages that were required. Indeed, there is proof that British Railways were already deploying signboards at some AHB locations with just the 'IN EMERGENCY – PHONE SIGNALMAN' message, long before the Hixon collision occurred. Certainly this seems to have been the case at Leominster AHB crossing where in a photograph taken in the autumn of 1966, prior to the 8 November incident, a signboard with the truncated message is clearly visible mounted above the telephone on the light mast, orientated to face parallel to the carriageway, where someone stranded on the crossing would stand most chance of seeing it (*see* plate 2). It came out during the Hixon Inquiry, in the cross-examination of Mr F. M. Hale, the Ministry of Transport's signage expert, that because Leominster crossing was on a trunk road, the A49, choice of which signs were most appropriate to use was under the control, not of Colonel Reed and the Inspectorate, but of Mr F. S. Alexander of the Ministry's Roads Engineering Division. Therefore, Leominster had separation of the message on the dual-purpose signboard, and this was a considerable bone of contention between Reed and Alexander, as Reed considered the dual-purpose signboard perfectly adequate. In fact Reed gave as his opinion during his lengthy cross-examination during the Hixon Inquiry, that the more signs there were at a crossing the greater the likelihood that none of them would be successful in transmitting any information, because motorists would become confused. Alexander on the other hand recognized that drivers of 'exceptional' vehicles needed advance warning of the need to phone the signalman before crossing the lines, a signboard virtually on the crossing, as prescribed by Reed was ... virtually useless.

Now, I knew that what I have written about the Leominster incident was the truth, as best as I could recall it. Imagine my surprise therefore, when having retired in 2012, I decided to investigate the matter more closely and quickly established that there was indeed a near-miss at Leominster on 8 November 1966, exactly as my father had described it, except that his part in it *was not mentioned at all* and that, moreover, the Leominster incident itself was not reported upon *until it came up in, and was central to*, the findings and recommendations of the *Hixon Inquiry Report*, published in July1968. My father died in 2000, so, unfortunately, I was unable to reconfirm his version of events. However, the internet has transformed our ability to access information and therefore the first investigatory step I took was to type 'Leominster', 'level-crossing' and '1966' into 'search' and this straight away directed me to the *Hixon Inquiry Report*, which is available in full, on line, published by railwayarchive. I read through it with increasing excitement, coupled with perplexity, because I knew that the version of events at Leominster as they were described in the Report, and my father's story, differed markedly and could not both be true.

When I write 'central to the findings and recommendations of the Hixon Inquiry', that, if anything proved to be an understatement; for example, one intriguing thing the incident at Leominster and the Hixon tragedy had in common, other than both taking place at recently installed automatic level-crossings, was that the road haulage firm involved at both occurrences was the same: Robert Wynn and Sons Limited, of Newport, Monmouthshire (usually known by their abbreviated title of Wynns). As quickly became clear when I began to examine the archived inquiry documents, Wynns' presence in both instances, was pivotal to the way that British Railways and more particularly the Railway Inspectorate, chose to present their case as to how and why the Hixon accident had occurred: in short they sought to blame Wynns. This course of action, and its subsequent partial unravelling led directly to Finding No. 7 of the *Hixon Inquiry Report* that states:

> The principal faults of British Railways contributing to the accident [at Hixon] were: (a) their failure when replying to a letter of the 19th November 1966, relating to an alarming incident at an automatic crossing at Leominster, to inform Robert Wynn and Sons Limited of the imperative necessity for drivers of heavy transport to comply with the telephone procedure ...

As I was to discover, first British Railways, and then the Railway Inspectorate, attempted to pin complete responsibility on to Robert Wynn and Sons Limited, for both the Leominster incident and the Hixon disaster, and it was this attempt, and its partial apprehension by the Chairman of the Hixon Inquiry, that, paradoxically, resulted in my father's part in preventing a catastrophe at Leominster being concealed.

The chairman appointed for the Hixon Inquiry was Mr E. Brian Gibbens QC, the Recorder of Oxford, who had, during 1967, presided over a judicial public inquiry into 'The Administration of Punishment at Court Lees Approved School', an innocuous sounding title, which masked the considerable effect of that inquiry's findings: initially, immediate closure of Court Lees Approved School, but, more importantly, the first really objective examination of the use of corporal punishment within the UK state school system as a whole. Gibbens's role in the 'Court Lees affair' had received much comment, both positive and negative, in the national press, and he was linked, by the press, to the reforming agenda of Roy Jenkins MP, the then Home Secretary, who had appointed him to investigate Court Lees Approved School. (Gibbens was also counsel for members of the National Union of Mineworkers at the Tribunal into the Aberfan disaster of 21 October 1966; this experience seems to have affected him quite profoundly, particularly as far as the potential in such tragically charged situations for scapegoats to be looked for was concerned.)

So, Gibbens was chosen to take charge of the Hixon proceedings, primarily because he had already ably demonstrated with the Court Lees Inquiry that he was not afraid to take on vested interests in order to get at the truth of a situation, and not merely because he had no professional connection with the railway industry.

Unlike, of course, the Railway Inspectorate, which as its name implies was intimately connected with all aspects of the railways in this country and notably, since the mid-1950s, had been closely involved in the preparatory work towards, and the subsequent introduction of, automatic crossings. Two men in particular, Colonels Denis McMullen and W. P. Reed were directly connected to both Hixon and Leominster. McMullen was, from 1963, the Chief Inspecting Officer, with overall responsibility for all aspects of railway safety, and Reed had operational charge of AHB crossing installations from November 1961 onwards, and had therefore overseen the installations at both Hixon and Leominster. Moreover, both men were heavily involved in the research and planning for the introduction of the new crossings, having led separate fact-finding trips to the Netherlands and France in 1956 and 1961, to see train-activated level-crossings in action. It is fair to say that these two Inspecting Officers were at the very heart of introducing automatic level-crossings into this country. The view was taken by the Minister of Transport, Barbara Castle, that it would have been very difficult for an Inspecting Officer to hold an inquiry into Hixon, because it could have been said that the Railway Inspectorate was investigating the decisions of the Railway Inspectorate. In reaching this view, Mrs Castle would have received advice from her Ministry's Under-Secretary for the Railways Group, Mr C. P. Scott-Malden, another man who had been deeply involved in the introduction of AHB crossings into this country, and who now found himself in day-to-day charge of part of a Ministry, most of whose numerous sub-divisions had made important contributions towards the automation of level-crossings, and which now therefore would come under intense scrutiny during the Hixon

Inquiry. (There is intriguing documentary evidence of a considerable tussle within the Ministry as to whether the Railway Inspectorate should nonetheless have put forward to investigate the Hixon collision, which will be looked at in the following chapter.)

The role that Mr Scott-Malden played and the actions that he took in shaping the Ministry of Transport's response to the inquiry, and consequently to its eventual outcome, were considerable; and his carefully calculating approach is now instantly recognizable to all those familiar with the fictional Whitehall mandarin, Sir Humphrey Appleby, in the television situation comedy *Yes Minister*. Although, of course, the circumstances pertaining to the Hixon Inquiry were no laughing matter.

Also, there was another reason why the Railway Inspectorate would probably have proved unsuitable to investigate Hixon, which was that, unlike most previous railway accidents, where the relevant personnel involved were almost exclusively railway employees, this was not the case at Hixon; the investigation here would require an ability and a willingness to deal even-handedly with a private company, Wynns, who initially at least, were suspected of the most grievous and negligent incompetence in their operating procedures. The inquisitorial procedures of the Railway Inspectorate, an anomaly within the British governmental and legal systems (more akin to the French Investigating Magistracy than anything else on this side of the Channel) were seen, at the time, to be unsuitable for the task of investigating what had happened on 6 January 1968.

Gibbens, as Chairman of the Inquiry, was to be supported by two assessors, Brigadier Richard Gardiner and Mr Grenville Berry, both men expert in their particular field: Gardiner, a former Royal Engineer railway specialist in India, during the Second World War and afterwards, and Berry, a leading civil engineer, specializing in road signage and signals. (One of the expert witnesses at the inquiry, Mr Colin Buchanan, Professor of Transport at Imperial College, London, also provided considerable technical assistance, as well as several remarkably penetrating insights into the mind-set of those in charge of the AHB crossing installation programme.)

Throughout the spring and early summer of 1968 the Hixon Inquiry gathered evidence, took testimony and examined witnesses; as mentioned previously, Gibbens's considerable brief was not only to investigate the accident at Hixon, but also to assess the introduction of automatic level-crossings across the country, and to make recommendations. The Railway Inspectorate, for once, were among those being scrutinized, rather than being the scrutineers.

It was this broader remit of the examination of the installation of all automatic level-crossings in the country, and the attendant publicity that this produced, that gave the opportunity for much information and testimony to be put forward, which probably would not have come to light if the investigation had been conducted by the Railway Inspectorate alone, using their tried and tested methodology of focusing intensively upon the facts of each particular accident. Quite why a review of the entire process of the installation of automatic crossings was specified as part of the Hixon Inquiry might seem self-evident: a deeply perturbing accident had occurred at one of many, only quite recently installed innovatory crossings, and it was therefore imperative to find out as soon as possible if there was a generic problem, or problems, with them, that might lead to further such accidents.

It is also the case that even before the Hixon collision there was some disquiet concerning the AHB crossings, or 'continental crossings' as they were usually styled, being aired in newspapers, not just the national papers but in the regional and local press as well; for example the Labour MP for Belper, the vocal and ebullient George Brown, was quoted in the *Derby Evening Telegraph*, as describing the situation at one of the new crossings in his constituency as 'utter madness' as early as 1964. He led a deputation to the Ministry of Transport at the time, which was told that, 'as long as the correct procedure was carried out by the public there was no danger'. (This was before the 1964 General Election that saw Labour returned to power and Brown made a member of the Cabinet, as Deputy Prime Minister.)

Of course, after the Hixon collision there was an immediate and intensive media interest in the workings of the new crossings, some of it very well informed and not at all sensational, some less so. Certainly few motorists would now have been unaware of the existence of the AHB crossings and the need to treat them with due caution; but in the last analysis, this reactive media coverage was a poor substitute for a properly thought-out and targeted public information campaign, from those in the Ministry of Transport, who were responsible for imposing the new crossings on a largely unsuspecting nation.

At this point an examination of precisely why the new crossings were being introduced is necessary: 'In order to save time and money', is the short but perfectly adequate answer. The old gated crossings took several minutes to complete a closing and opening cycle (with the heavy wooden gates either being moved manually, or by means of a hand-turned mechanism) and what with the countrywide increase in vehicular traffic post-war, it was felt that the new crossings with their operating cycle of around thirty seconds, would be a vast improvement. In particular it was believed that the automatic crossings would ease traffic congestion on the road network as a whole, which would lead to fewer accidents and thereby fewer deaths and injuries. The main monetary cost of the gated crossings lay in the huge wage bill for the crossing-keepers needed to keep them functioning across the country, and many of them around the clock: approximately a billion pounds per annum in today's money. Each AHB crossing cost £7,000 to install, as opposed to an annual on-cost of £3,000 for each existing manned crossing, so the financial case for automation seemed compelling and unanswerable. The statistical case for time saved by automation was also strong: paragraph 242 of the *Hixon Inquiry Report*, approvingly quoting the Ministry of Transport, says:

> Not only does the automatic barrier provide a shorter time of closure, but because of its rapid operation it may be opened and closed far more frequently than the old type of crossing, with the result that the impediment to road traffic is for, say, three short periods, whereas previously it would have been for one long closure extending over twice the total time of those three brisk operations ... The Netherlands Railways have established that at a busy level-crossing where there are frequent trains, automatic operation reduces the loss of time for road traffic by 75 per cent and, furthermore, 75 per cent of the traffic which would previously have had to wait is not now interrupted at all.

So, there was no real argument over whether AHB crossings should be introduced; however, it was how they were to be introduced that does not seem to have been adequately considered by the Ministry of Transport. Moreover, the reliance on the model provided by the Netherlands' introduction of AHB crossings is evident in this quotation; the sub-text being, if it works for the Dutch, why should it not work for us?

Also, as came out during the Hixon Inquiry, there were concerns within the railway industry that it was increasingly difficult to recruit suitable staff for the crossing-keepers' work, because the job required conscientiousness and attention to detail, particularly the ability to stay alert during long periods of inactivity, all this for comparatively little financial reward. It was a Victorian-era task which still needed doing in the 1960s, an age that was self-consciously seeking to embrace all aspects of modernity. Moreover, 'getting rid of the human element' in railway operating systems had long been believed to decrease the likelihood of accidents; over 120 years cumulative experience of systematically investigating such accidents had convinced the men of the Railway Inspectorate of the strength of this axiom. Therefore, introducing automatic level-crossings was seen as being not only cheaper and more efficient, but was *bound* to be safer as well. This viewpoint had been reinforced for Colonel Reed, when he had been the investigating inspector at a particularly blatant instance of human error causing an accident at a conventional crossing. This was at Roundstone level-crossing near Angmering on the Brighton to Portsmouth line that occurred on 22 September 1965. An Electrical Multiple Unit hit a double-decker bus on the crossing and carried it fifty-four yards along the tracks. A fire broke out and spread rapidly through the bus, leaving three dead and eight injured among the bus passengers. The crossing-keeper thought he had missed a train going by – it was foggy – and he opened the crossing gates to road traffic, then the train came along, travelling at around 35 mph. Reed in his report stated that the accident could not have happened if the crossing had been converted to AHB status, which, as he put it, 'only requires simple obedience from the road user' to ensure safe operation.

The models for the new crossings were to be found already operating on the Continental and North American railway systems, and it was believed that, to a large extent, Britain could 'cherry-pick' the best elements from other countries' work and experience. However the flip-side of this is that, as the *Hixon Inquiry Report* points out, the fact-finding tours of the Continent of 1956 and 1961 concluded that the AHB crossings they had seen were 'proved successful' and that therefore there was no real attempt to 'think things out intensively from the very beginning' (paragraph 56). The use of automatic crossings in the Netherlands was seen as a particularly appropriate model for this country. One distinctive aspect of the working of the Dutch AHB crossings was that none of them had telephones for the use of the public. By contrast, it had been decided to put telephones for the use of the public, to contact the covering signal box, into the barriers of the British automatic crossings as the standard installation procedure, when they were first introduced from 1961 onwards. The early accompanying signboards merely stated: 'Use telephone if there is undue delay', presumably a delay in the barriers rising after a train had gone past. Therefore, it never really crystallized in anybody's mind why those phones might prove essential either for the safe *routine* use of the new crossings in Britain, or in the event of an emergency situation. Instead, perversely in a way, the plain fact that the Dutch crossings operated without telephones seems to have been *all* that crystallized in one man's mind, and that was Colonel Reed of the Railway Inspectorate. Certainly, Reed, who was in charge of AHB crossing introduction from late 1961, was extremely impressed with what he saw in operation abroad, particularly with the Netherlands State Railways' introduction of automation, and the cogent and well-executed nature of publicity associated with the switch to the 'robot' crossings in the Netherlands. In his evidence to the Hixon Inquiry he was fulsome in his praise for what he regarded as the obvious way forward for Britain's railways:

> The numerous examples which we saw in Holland of the manner in which delays to road traffic were reduced to a minimum by auto–half-barrier equipment at busy crossings in built-up areas, adjacent to railway stations … at busy crossings on high-speed important roads … with heavy rail traffic … The general opinion [in Holland] was that almost any crossing was suitable for AHB working.

Colonel Reed was entirely convinced of the efficacy of the Dutch approach and he seems to have believed it could be imported into this country virtually intact and with no real need for further assessment. The proof of this is that he pushed for the removal of restrictions on speed of trains and for consideration of a much broader range of sites for conversion. Moreover, and most significantly it was on Reed's 'watch' that legislation was introduced to put in AHB crossings with no barrier phones for the use of the public. That would, indeed, could never, have happened if anybody had considered the full range of traffic likely to be using the new installations in this country, but that 'first principle' analysis never took place, instead the chimera of emulating the Dutch fixed itself in Reed's mind.

An interesting objective question to ask is, what steps did the Dutch authorities take if abnormal, that is very heavy, very large and very slow-moving, loads had to be moved on their road network? Well, not surprisingly, it being the Netherlands, they insisted most such abnormal work was done using the canal system, but for the inevitable cases where unusually slow and heavy indivisible loads had to be moved across AHB crossings the Rijksdienst voor het wegerkeer (Ministry of Transport) issued a permit to the hauliers concerned, who then had to contact the state railways at least a week in advance to negotiate an agreed transit. The simple key to having safe movements without barrier telephones was putting a system into place, where for the small but predictable number of special permit movements, the Dutch hauliers had been informed about what was required of them, and the Railway had to have staff on hand to contact the covering signal-box via a walkie-talkie radio. Strange as it may seem, this method of operating AHB crossings *without* telephones for the use of the public was pursued by the Railway Inspectorate after the Hixon collision and proposed in their considered response to the Hixon Inquiry, as one way forward for automatic crossings in Britain *with* telephones for the use of the public; it was given short shrift by Chairman Gibbens in paragraph 305 of the *Hixon Inquiry Report*: 'It seems to me that at first sight, either it is necessary for safety to have the railway employee present, or it is not.' With that pithy comment he summed up the essential consideration that underpinned the introduction of AHB crossings, which the Inspectorate apparently had still not yet fully grasped, which seems unlikely. Or more plausibly, that even after the Hixon collision the Inspectorate was engaged in exploring ways in which automatic crossings might operate, without telephones for the use of the public.

It is worth noting that it was the perceptive expert witness, Professor Colin Buchanan, who in his statement to the inquiry, first made the point that Gibbens expounds on in paragraph 305. Buchanan also said in his statement that his first impression of AHB crossings in action was that they, 'looked dangerous and felt dangerous'.

Chapter 2

The legal stuff and the Men from The Ministry

B rian Gibbens QC, seems in retrospect a very astute choice for overseeing the onerous task of finding out what had happened at Hixon and examining the introduction of AHB crossings into Britain; not only had he successfully chaired a high-profile inquiry into alleged brutality at Court Lees Approved School in 1967, but he had also been the leading counsel for the National Union of Mineworkers and the Colliery Officials and Staffs Association, at the harrowing Aberfan Disaster Tribunal of 1966. He was fifty-six years old in 1968 and was apparently noted for his courteous and dryly humorous courtroom manner and, judging from a photograph taken at the time of the Hixon Inquiry, he bore more than a passing resemblance to the actor, the late Pete Postlethwaite.

Gibbens was from Staffordshire and attended Newcastle-under-Lyme High School and then the egalitarian St Catherine's Society, at the University of Oxford, which provided a means by which able students of limited means could gain a degree. Gibbens must have been exceptionally able, because he became a barrister in 1934, at the comparatively youthful age of twenty-two. During the Hixon Inquiry hearings, he let slip his wartime service in the Royal Artillery, when he admonished Colonel Reed for failing to take any account of the local surroundings of each proposed AHB crossing: 'In the last war, when I was pretending to be a gunner, we were taught to use every God-given piece of information we could glean from the surrounding countryside.' It was whilst he was in the Royal Artillery that he met Roy Jenkins, who he probably served with at the Enigma code-breakers HQ, Bletchley Park.

As well as chairing the Court Lees Inquiry and his experience at the Aberfan Tribunal, Gibbens had also been in charge of a tribunal into conditions at a psychiatric hospital in Oxfordshire, for the local Health Board, in 1966. So, a clever and appropriately experienced lawyer, sure of himself in a courtroom, particularly *his* courtroom, as was to become apparent. On 29 January 1968, the first day of the proceedings, Gibbens made absolutely clear what he regarded his inquiry's relationship to the Ministry of Transport, and indeed the whole machinery of Government to be: 'The chairman explained that although the inquiry was appointed under the Transport Minister's warrant it was entirely independent, and it could, if it thought fit, examine the actions of any Government department.' (*Morning Star*, 30/01/68) Gibbens was aware that the findings of his inquiry would have the force of statute behind them: the Minister of Transport, and the Ministry which served her would be obliged to not only take notice of what the Hixon Inquiry said, but to follow its recommendations. (This was in contrast to any inquiry and report by the Railway Inspectorate, which had only ever had advisory status and whose recommendations could be ignored, if for example they were thought to be too expensive or onerous to implement; an infamous example of just this happening, is of course the Inspectorate's advice that an automatic emergency braking system should be made universal on Britain's railways, made in the early 1950s and not acted upon until the 1980s, after numerous fatal accidents over the intervening years, which probably would not have occurred if the Inspectorate's recommendations had been followed.)

However, there remained the possibility that if Gibbens's inquiry could be shown to be demonstrably failing in discharging its responsibilities, say by taking an inordinately long time to reach a conclusion, or by clearly not getting to grips with the considerable technical issues involved, then in those circumstances the Minister of Transport might be persuaded to set it aside and rely instead upon the recommendations of a brand-new policy document on the subject of the automation of railway level-crossings produced by the Ministry of Transport. Because the production of just such a document was ordered by Under-Secretary Scott-Malden, and moreover, barely three weeks into the hearings for the Hixon Inquiry he attempted to pull the rug from under Gibbens with a thoroughgoing assault on the competency and progress of the inquiry to date, in a detailed internal memorandum dated 14 March 1968, and intended primarily for his Minister, Barbara Castle. The reason he wrote this extraordinary missive was that something had gone terribly wrong with Scott-Malden's courtroom strategy for the Ministry during the inquiry and, as we shall see, it related to the events at Leominster on 8 November 1966. The Secretary to the Inquiry, W. Patrick Jackson, responded to Scott-Malden's memorandum defending the Inquiry's rate of progress and revealing that he had already had a lengthy verbal argument with a senior official in the Inspectorate over whether a public inquiry was suitable for investigating the Hixon disaster. Clearly, battle lines were being drawn amongst those conducting the inquiry itself!

The dual task in front of Gibbens's inquiry in January 1968 was on the face of it complex, the Hixon accident itself had to be investigated, alongside the larger and overarching questioning of the use of automatic level-crossings on Britain's railway network. Gibbens decided to deal with Hixon itself first, at least in terms of processing the witnesses and any written submissions. A month was allowed for those parties represented at the inquiry to get lists of witnesses and indications of their 'proofs' of evidence into the inquiry; also any interested parties were invited to submit their written opinions. (Some of the written 'proofs' were not presented to the inquiry, and therefore not available for all of the represented parties to peruse, until after the hearings were actually under way, which proved to be of tremendous import as to how the inquiry played out, and which put my father's actions on 8 November 1966 back onto centre stage). The broader investigation into the process of AHB crossing installation was to take place once the information specifically relating to the Hixon collision had been dealt with: that was the plan anyway, as long as events did not intervene to push the inquiry off course, of course …

It was not just that it was a Judge conducting the investigation into what had happened at Hixon rather than an Inspector of Railways, it was a completely different way of investigating. A court of inquiry is exactly that: a court of law, with an adversarial procedure of examining events which might admit to more than one possibility for their causation. The Hixon Inquiry was to generate over a million and a half words of written evidence and verbatim transcripts of the inquiry's proceedings, as the sixty-three witnesses were firstly taken through their written evidential 'proofs' by their own counsel, if they had one, or an inquiry counsel if they didn't, and were then available for cross-examination by the legal teams of other parties, under the experienced and watchful eye of the chairman of course. As recently as 1966, a Royal Commission under Lord Justice Salmon had laid down certain principles, but, instructively, no hard and fast rules, for what it termed 'inquisitorial inquiries' (but which were not really truly inquisitorial in the way that the Railway Inspectorates' investigations were).

Chairman Gibbens made it clear that the Hixon Inquiry would follow those principles, in particular the right for all parties likely to be criticized in the proceedings, to have notice of the allegations made against them, and to have adequate time to prepare their own case. In the light of this clear setting out of the rights of all those called in front of his inquiry, to have the best chance of making their case, there is a rather curious comment in paragraph 7 of the introduction to the *Hixon Inquiry Report* on there being 'two interesting features of the Inquiry', one being the fact that it was the first use of Section 7 of the Regulation of Railways Act, 1871 since the Tay Bridge Disaster Inquiry of 1880; and secondly this: 'the fact that the Ministry of Transport was separately represented at the hearings'.

This seems to be rather a throwaway comment to make in the circumstances, even a non sequitur; certainly, at the least, Gibbens clearly thought it worth pointing up, that although he had been charged with conducting the inquiry by the Ministry of Transport for the Minister of Transport, that Ministry then saw fit to maintain a separate legal status within proceedings, whilst the Inquiry was under way. The alternative would have been for the Inquiry's counsel to lead the seven Ministry of Transport witnesses through their evidence, which should have been perfectly acceptable, surely? After all, the situation was that both sets of barristers, the Ministry's and the Court of Inquiry's, were under instruction from, and in the charge of, the Government's legal officers, the

Treasury Solicitor's Department. That may have been the situation in theory, but the reality was quite different, as Ministry of Transport files containing minutes of meetings and memos relating to the inquiry and its conduct show clearly. Firstly, the Under-Secretary for the Railways Group at the Ministry, C. P. Scott-Malden, is revealed as the organizing genius, who presided over at least three, fully minuted briefing meetings for the seven Ministry witnesses who were to be called (and who knows how many un-minuted pep talks?). Scott-Malden had been an intelligence officer in the 1st Airborne Division during the war and had also achieved a double First at Cambridge; his stategy was straightforward, and can usefully be likened to the wartime naval convoy system: no aspect of Ministry of Transport staff's numerous interactions with AHB crossing installation was to be allowed to be 'picked off ' individually. As to its conduct, from the very start of the inquiry, the Ministry would ask to be judged as a unit. Moreover, each witness was coached on the best way to deliver their evidence, with this suggested felicitous phrase: 'An answer such as "With hindsight I can recognize that a number of those concerned, including myself, had the opportunity to recognize the abnormal load problem but did not do so" might suit the purpose.'

The seven key Ministry witnesses were colonels McMullen and Reed and Major Olver of the Railway Inspectorate, Mr A. D. Holland, responsible for routing abnormal Special Order loads, Mr J. R. Madge, head of the Road Safety Group, Mr F. D. Bickerton, head of Publicity at the Ministry and Scott-Malden himself, who was to answer on any policy decisions concerning AHB crossings not covered by the others. He advised his fellow witnesses to reference the setting out of the Ministry's position made on the opening day of the hearings: 'Under cross examination Ministry witnesses might well find it useful to refer back to statements made by Ministry counsel from the first day of the inquiry.' When for example, the Ministry's intention to ask to be judged collectively had been advanced succinctly by their leading counsel Mr Nigel Bridge QC: 'Such responsibility as the Ministry should properly bear, it accepts collectively.' By frequent repetition, Scott-Malden apparently hoped to persuade the Inquiry that no single individual from the Ministry could be pre-eminently blamed for the Hixon collision.

There was clearly then a well-prepared defensive position for the Ministry; Scott-Malden was very aware that individuals within the Ministry might find themseves heavily criticized for their actions as far as both the specific circumstances pertaining to the Hixon accident and the installation of AHB crossings generally were concerned. A three-page summary of areas of concern was produced, identifying over eighty ways in which the seven Ministry witnesses were advised of the likely questions they would be asked when they were cross-examined. Under-Secretary Scott-Malden certainly did his best to cover all the bases: he was not one for leaving things to chance if he could arrange things otherwise; and it must be admitted that in one regard at least, his careful preparations appear to have been entirely successful: the *Hixon Inquiry Report* does deliver its judgments on the Ministry collectively. Although Scott-Malden certainly did not think that it was a certainty that the Ministry would achieve this; at the briefing before the inquiry proper got under way, two days beforehand, on 27 February, he warned those present that they might find themselves in the position of having to admit to personal blame for the 'abnormal loads problem in particular'. So Scott-Malden realized that this was the area where individuals were likely to be picked off. He must have been very pleased that it did not happen. By the time of the last briefing on 20 May Scott-Malden allowed himself to sound almost up-beat: the Ministry counsel were going to make use of the 'very firm evidence of Flight Lieutenant Moreau' that the (dual purpose) signboard at Hixon crossing was 'at a reasonable angle of 26 degrees'. As we shall see, this 'very firm evidence' did effectively save the Ministry's bacon. (The press in their coverage of the hearings certainly picked up on how well drilled the Ministry witnesses were: 'as a team they were like a machine or a computer, through which came the evidence of a machine.' This was *The Journal*, Newcastle upon Tyne, 25/05/68 quoting the counsel for the Associated Society of Locomotive Engineers and Firemen, Mr Ronald Hopkins.)

Chairman Gibbens makes it clear that the introduction of AHB crossings, stretching back as it did to the mid-1950s, meant that some of those involved in decision-making had either retired or moved on, and therefore it would not be fair or equitable to apportion blame to individuals in the report's conclusions and recommendations. This did not mean, of course, that people's actions and decisions were not identified and attention drawn to them in the body of the report. One of Gibbens's favourite techniques in this respect was to quote extensively when a cross-examining counsel had made a particularly telling intervention, as with the unfortunate Mr Holland, who was responsible for Special Order routing. The following passage is quoted, when Holland was cross-examined by British Railways' barrister, Mr Fay:

Q: I suppose anyone with a pencil and paper and an elementary knowledge of mathematics can work out at what speed a vehicle of 150 feet long will get into danger on these crossings, if one knows the time factor between entering on a clear crossing and the earliest arrival of a train. Did no one in your Division ever work that out or bring it to your notice as a danger factor?

A: No.

There is a page and a half in the report devoted to more of this demolition of Holland's professional reputation (pages 58 and 59). However, all Gibbens really achieves by this sort of thing is to open up ways in which responsibility for the Hixon disaster can be spread around. If it was Everybody's fault then it quickly becomes Nobody's fault. In effect, Colonel Reed and the rest of the Inspectorate were able to hide behind the other departments of the Ministry; but theirs was the primary responsibility for installing and equipping the AHB crossings in an inadequate and dangerous fashion for the job they had to do. Everything else flowed from that. Chairman Gibbens never fully grasped that point, or rather, he did not keep it firmly in the forefront of his deliberations.

Instead he allowed the first part of the inquiry, into the actual accident, to become a rather frustrating and ultimately fruitless exercise in determining causality, with Wynns, Staffordshire Police, British Railways, the English Electric company and individual employees of all of them, being examined minutely to see what share of the blame they should take. Meanwhile, the Inspectorate were able to 'dissapear' into the camouflage of the Ministry of Transport, even though it was clear that it was the Inspectorate who had constructed the circumstances of the Hixon collision. It was their decisions which formed the *sine qua non* of the situation at Hixon and the other 197 AHB crossings on the rail network.

To summarize, Mr Scott-Malden wanted all of the departments of the Ministry of Transport to appear to be as helpful and co-operative with the inquiry as possible, whilst at the same time the Inspectorate were to produce a parallel and entirely separate set of proposals on AHB crossings, just in case the Ministry had to 'step into the breach' should the Inquiry itself come to be thought inadequate, for whatever reason. Coupled with this essentially defensive strategy, the Ministry's counsel at the inquiry were to carry out a ruthless attempt to blame all of the other parties involved in the Hixon accident for causing it, primarily Wynns, but also the police and even the Ministry's close partners, British Railways. Moreover, Scott-Malden may have thought that he had a useful 'spy in the camp' on behalf of the Ministry as far as the Inquiry went, in W. Patrick Jackson the Ministry official appointed as Secretary to the inquiry; however, Jackson proved to be very capable of making up his own mind as far as what he judged to be the best interests not of the Ministry, but of the country, as his trenchant 'open minutes' reveal. As discussed above, these were sent in its defence, when the Inquiry was attacked by Scott-Malden for being too time-consuming and burdensome. (Suffice to say that there is a lengthy and fascinating book to be written about the behind-the-scenes machinations and in-fighting at the Ministry of Transport, from the advent of the dynamic Ernest Marples MP, as Minister in the late 1950s through to the Ministry's abolition in 1970, but that is for another time.)

Finally in terms of key personnel at the Inquiry, we have the Treasury solicitor, Mr Cockburn, who was in charge of preparing the case for the Inquiry and instructing the Inquiry's counsel; possibly the most important part of his burdensome task was the calling of the sixty-three witnesses who actually spoke at the inquiry and the marshalling of their statements of evidence, or 'proofs', together with further 'proofs' from potential further witnesses. One of these, a statement from a Mr Leslie Lloyd, Movements Manager of British Railways Western Region, which detailed what had occurred at Leominster level-crossing on 8 November 1966, as far as the Railway was aware, was what turned the tables on the Railway Inspectorate's attempt to off-load responsibility for problems with AHB crossings onto other parties. (Although Lloyd was a Movements Manager on Western Region, his statement of evidence uses the phrase 'as far as the Board is concerned'. This is significant because it indicates his statement was made with the approval of British Railways' national management, not just Lloyd's superiors on Western Region; if they were consulted at all. Somebody was determined to point out that Colonel Reed was in full possession of the facts as to both the condition of the road approaches at Leominster crossing, together with an account of the most significant safety-related event that had occured there since it had been converted to automatic working. And yet Reed had signed it off as fit and safe for use after inspecting it on 23 February 1967.)

Presumably, British Railways would have been anxious to provide a truthful account to the Inquiry of everything that they were aware of concerning the installation of AHB crossing. However, there exists an intriguing letter from British Railways chief legal adviser, Mr M. H. B. Gilmour, addressed to the Railway Inspectorate at the Ministry of Transport. Part of the content of this frankly rather exasperated letter, reveals exactly why British Railways wanted to make certain, via Leslie Lloyd's witness statement, that Colonel Reed was identified as having been fully aware of the unsatisfactory state of the southern road approach to the Leominster crossing: 'since Colonel McMullen has now criticized the Board for opening this crossing before these roadworks were completed'. In other words, British Railways were making sure that they were not blamed by the Chief Inspecting Officer of Railways (McMullen) for allowing the crossing to operate, when that decision had actually been taken by one of his own senior colleagues. The letter is dated 28 March 1968, and is mainly asking for information on the Leominster crossing roadworks, which had been promised a fortnight beforehand. As an indication of how seriously British Railways' chief legal adviser was taking the evidence-gathering process for the Inquiry, he makes a point of stating explicitly that he is sending a copy of his letter to Mr Cockburn, the Treasury solicitor overseeing the evidence-gathering process. Of course, this also indicates a certain lack of trust between British Railways and the Railway Inspectorate. As it turns out, Colonel McMullen's witness statement seems to have refrained from criticizing British Railways for operating the Leominster crossing, because clearly that decision, along with so much else concerning AHB crossings, was Colonel Reed's.

On a much wider issue, relating to how the new crossings were to be introduced to the national consciousness Mr Gilmour's letter also asks for the Ministry to provide a copy of a letter dating from October 1957, that is, just after the automation process had been given approval. In this early correspondence, the Ministry had stated that they would be contacting the RAC and the AA together with the Road Haulage Association (RHA) to keep them abreast of developments as far as AHB crossings were concerned, so therefore British Railways need not bother. This is interesting for two reasons: firstly, because there is no evidence that the Ministry ever did keep these three road-vehicle users' organizations abreast of developments, they never, for example, notified them of the 1963 change in legislation that telephones, for the use of the public in emergencies, were no longer to be installed as standard at the new crossings. That kind of information might have had a galvanizing effect on *somebody* in one of the organizations to question the wisdom of this change, but they were never given the chance. Secondly, the reason that British Railways was asking for a copy of the 1957 letter from the Ministry, was to bring to the Hixon Inquiry's attention that the Ministry appeared to have overlooked this particular piece of interesting correspondence in its submissions to the Inquiry.

In point of fact the A.A. and R.A.C. joint consultative committee was only contacted once or twice about AHB crossings by the Ministry, and that was in 1957 and 1958, when things were regarded as being at an 'experimental' stage; and long before the first automatic crossing was installed in 1961.

Chapter 3

Murphy's Law, or the Engineer's Touchstone

If something can go wrong, it will go wrong, especially if it is merely a matter of enough trials of a system.

What became clear following the Hixon collision, was that the truly revolutionary alteration in responsibility for safety at public vehicular-access level-crossings, alluded to in chapter 1, had not been thought through in its implications. Because, make no mistake, the thinking behind the introduction of automation relied upon the British public, specifically drivers of motor vehicles accepting an entirely new safety relationship between themselves and the Railways. Since 1839, legislation had required the operators of the railways to maintain 'good and sufficient' gates kept normally closed against the road, effectively fencing the railways in. However, as the volume of road traffic increased for most level-crossings, exceptions to this rule were allowed, by permission of the President of the Board of Trade (and after 1919 by the Ministry of Transport) so that the gates were normally open to the road and closed across the railway tracks. Also, the gates for the majority of manned crossings, certainly those on main lines, were interlocked with protecting railway signals, so that these could only be set at 'clear' for trains once the gates had been shut against the road. A 'belt-and-braces' system that both the railwaymen who operated it and the public understood and trusted. The simple truth was that for well over a century the people of the United Kingdom, uniquely in the world, had got used to the operators of the railways being responsible for closing off, behind those reassuringly solid gates, the railway tracks, whilst a train was passing over a level-crossing. Crucially, the burden of responsibility for ensuring public safety, was seen to rest firmly with the operators of the railways, and moreover, the general public had an expectation that a road vehicle would not be allowed on to a level-crossing if a train was about to occupy it. Now, quite rapidly, this belief was being negated, as up and down the country automatic level-crossings were installed: by December 1967 there were 198 entirely automatic and unmanned level-crossings in place and operational. At these crossings, all that stood between the road user and the railway was a deliberately flimsy barrier across one half of the roadway, the final decision as to whether to proceed onto the tracks in front of them was now entirely in the hands of members of the public.

Not that those with the primary responsibility for the safe functioning of automatic crossings were unaware of this fundamental adjustment: the Railway Inspectorate, in a submission to Parliament in 1957, clearly stated what the situation would become: 'With the introduction of lifting barriers at level-crossings, and in particular if automatic half-barriers are to be adopted, the principle must be recognised that it is the responsibility of the individual to protect himself from the hazards of the railway in the same way as from the hazards of the road ...'

One of the main supporting justifications for shifting this primary duty of care away from the railway onto the vehicle-using general public, was that pedestrians had always been responsible for not putting themselves in front of an oncoming train, via wicket gates and over unsupervised crossings, for as long as the railways had been in existence. It was therefore seen as a logical and necessary step for the drivers of motor vehicles of all types and sizes to assume the same primary responsibility for not taking their vehicle onto a crossing if it was indicated that it was unsafe to do so. What was not appreciated was the psychological complexity of the shift for vehicle drivers from being prevented physically from moving forward (and then when they were allowed to proceed, the gates that had been obstructing them being put back in place across the railway tracks, thereby demonstrating physically that it was safe to proceed) to the new situation where, first of all they had to decide whether to stop or not, and then whether to remain stationary, or to drive around the descended barrier in front of them, and finally whether to move forward onto the crossing when it was indicated that they had permission to do so (with the railway lines now clearly open on either side of them, as they drove over the crossing). The individual motorist's experience of moving their vehicle from one side of a railway line to the other had altered, from the certainty of a cattle-like wait of a few minutes in front of a solid wooden gate, shutting them off from the railway and requiring no real decision on their part, to the possibility of a complex, permissive interaction demanding at least three separate 'stop'/'go' choices, all to be completed within around thirty to forty seconds. Hopefully, all present-day motorists would say, that when faced with flashing lights and ringing bells at a level-crossing, there is not really any question of choice as to whether or not to proceed: we have *learned* what to do. (Those in the Railway Inspectorate considering the possible occurrences at the new crossings became almost entirely focused on the likelihood, as they saw it, of impatient motorists zigzagging around the half-barrier if they were kept waiting for too long. The possible presence of nervous and uncertain drivers waiting anxiously for the barriers to lift, was never really addressed.) As far as the other side of this complex, permissive interaction was concerned something equally profound had occurred, but which was only really obvious to those involved in bringing it about; the role of 'the Railway' had morphed from physically imposing a single indivisible procedure – of the crossing keeper placing the heavy gates first, across the entire width of the road and then back across the entire width of the railway – to merely indicating withdrawal of permission to cross the railway line (lights flashing and bells ringing, half-barriers fall), followed by an indication of the re-instatement of that permission (lights cease flashing and bells cease ringing, half-barriers rise). In the *Hixon Inquiry Report* the rationale for the introduction of automatic crossings was summed up in the following sentence: 'In the presence of modern technology the old gates were a creaking anachronism.' This view seems eminently reasonable, looking back from a distance of nearly fifty years when the public has had ample time to adjust to the operation of automatic crossings, but, and it is a considerable 'but', that even by the late 1960s this familiarization and learning process had scarcely begun. Indeed, the significance of the profound change in behaviour that was being required of vehicle drivers, was again, never really addressed by those in charge of the process of automation.

Because, those in the Railway Inspectorate and Ministry of Transport primarily responsible for the introduction of the new technology had given little consideration as to how they might manage the Great British Public's introduction to the new reality; where the choice of whether to proceed onto the crossing was entirely in the hands of a road user, *who more likely than not* still thought that 'the Railway' would not allow a train to run onto a crossing if there was a vehicle already on it; just as the situation had been for the previous century or so, with the old fully gated crossings. From their testimony to the Hixon Inquiry, it is clear that the lorry drivers involved at both Leominster and Hixon, believed that once a road vehicle was on a level-crossing that 'there must be something in the mechanism to put the signal at stop to the train', as Mr James Horton, the driver at Leominster put it. Mr Bryn Groves, the driver of the leading tractor unit at Hixon, stated plainly, 'Whilst on the crossing I did not think the barrier could be set in operation.' At the time, that tragically mistaken belief would undoubtedly have been shared by the vast majority of the British vehicle-driving public.

Now however, the situation on the new automatic crossings, was transformed, in that the heavy wooden gates closing off the railway entirely, were replaced by lifting, single-carriageway-only obstructing barriers. These were set into operation by an approaching train's wheels 'shorting out' a very low voltage current (less than half a volt) that was passed through the rails themselves. This switching system was supplemented by the flanges of the leading set of wheels on the locomotive 'striking in' physically to twin mechanical treadles, positioned close to the inside of both rails, thereby switching on an electrical current which travelled through armoured copper-wire cable (around an inch thick) laid alongside the railway tracks, to the crossing, about 1,000 yards distant. Immediately, warning bells and lights on the crossing would ring and flash and eight seconds later the barriers would begin to fall, being fully lowered around eight seconds after that. Then, if it was an express, the train would be on the crossing in a further eight seconds. In effect, the new AHB crossings were straightforward enough electro-mechanical devices, the initiating switch mechanisms (the circuit breakers and the treadles) of which, were separated from the moving, flashing and ringing, 'slave' components, by quite large, but not inordinate, distances. In the best traditions of railway engineering safety the dual switching systems were seen as (another) 'belt-and-braces' solution: if one system failed the other would work. The essential thing was that the barriers came down. The AHB mechanisms were designed to 'fail-to-safe' in virtually all conditions; that is, if there was an electrical current failure, then the barriers were deliberately weighted so that they would fall across the road carriageway. Although there were numerous 'fail-to-safe' incidents up and down the country there were few 'fail-to-danger' occurrences between 1964 and 1967, when the 'spike' in AHB installations was taking place.

Deliberately, no provision had been made to protect the revolutionary new crossings with signals. Therefore, if any road vehicle, having once started onto the crossing, was unable to complete its journey through having stalled or become obstructed – should the barriers come down – the occupants would have less than ten seconds to get clear of the crossing. Of course, this unfortunate sequence of events was judged to be unlikely to occur, most of the time. Most of the time, it was calculated, in what was thought to be the statistically very remote possibility of a vehicle being stuck on a crossing, there would be no train due precipitately. Therefore, a stalled car could be restarted, or failing that pushed off the crossing, and if the vehicle was too large to be pushed off then a phone call could be made to the covering signal-box, from the phone prudently installed in, or close to, the barrier mechanism; if it had been so installed, of course, because between early 1963 and October,1966 such phones were not standard for all AHB crossings, and they were not retrospectively fitted to those without them until after the recommendations of the Hixon Inquiry. (Nearly ten percent of AHB crossings had no phones installed in, or adjacent to, the barriers as of January 1968.)

The question of how likely it was that a vehicle would stall on a level-crossing, was calculated by treating the length of carriageway (around twelve yards) through each crossing as though it was merely exactly equivalent to any other similar length of carriageway on the 200,000 miles of the British road network. On this basis it was decided that the possibility of anyone stalling on one of the new AHB crossings was remote, so remote that it could be dismissed, virtually out of hand (just as Mr Lattimer, Assistant General

Manager of British Railways, Western Region, did in his letter of response to Wynns of 29 November 1966).

The men of the Railway Inspectorate, who oversaw the introduction of the new crossings, knew that they were producing a system that would, in all probability, cost some lives at the unfamiliar AHB crossings. However, they were of the opinion that their new system would – on balance – actually save lives elsewhere on the road network, because it would reduce road traffic congestion and therefore the number of collisions and casualties due to that congestion. They were supported into this belief (seduced might be a better description) by official actuarial statistical tables, which emphasized the huge disparity between total UK road casualties and casualties at level-crossings; in the mid-sixties the yearly average for road deaths was just below 8,000, whilst controlled level-crossing fatalities were usually in single figures, eight being the annual average for 1961–7.

This minor, 'playing God' aspect of their work does not seem to have troubled the Railway Inspectorate at all; in fact, quite the reverse, and reducing traffic congestion by getting the vehicle waiting time at level-crossings down to as short a span as possible seems to have become something of an obsession. Trains were to operate at their maximum possible speed when approaching the new crossings, so that with an express travelling at 90 mph, the time between its 'striking in' and its appearance on the crossing was reduced to a scant twenty-four seconds. Six seconds after the last pair of wheels on the train left the crossing, the train would have 'struck out' and the automatic barriers would be upright again, all done and dusted in around half a minute.

There was, of course, another reason for this emphasis on speed, in that the vehicle-driving public were to be taught by object lesson that they should not try to 'beat the crossing', by either racing under a descending barrier, or nipping around the side of a descended one. The view was taken by the Railway Inspectorate, in particular by Colonel Reed, who was in charge of the AHB crossing installation programme from late 1961, that the best way of educating the public as to how the new crossings worked, was through drivers experiencing them in action; people would rapidly learn, after observing once or twice, how quickly a train appeared in front of them, that they should stay put, and that then they would soon be safely on their way again. It was the use of the 'implacable velocity' of the train's approach to the crossing that was to instil the necessary discipline in road users. As early as 1957, in the initial submissions to Parliament regarding the introduction of automatic crossings, it was made clear that, 'the object of the short time is that very quickly the public know that there is no chance of beating the thing. When the barrier comes down, it means a train is there, and there is no temptation to beat it. If we attempt to link up with the signals, we almost certainly lose the discipline of the public, I think'.

Further on in the same submission we have this: 'that if, when an emergency arose, the train had passed the last signal at which it could be arrested, nothing could be done to stop the train before it reached the crossing'. The choice was made to not 'link up' the new crossings with the railway signalling system. Thus, the new automatic level-crossings began to be installed from the early 1960s, in the knowledge that they had no integral 'fail-safe' system. If an emergency situation arose on a crossing, then, if there was sufficient time and if barrier phones had been fitted, a phone call to the supervising signal-box *might* be able to stop any trains arriving on the crossing whilst it was obstructed; but in the unfortunate situation where a train had already passed any potential warning signal, then a signalman was powerless, and once it had 'shorted out' and 'struck in' to the treadles which activated the AHB mechanism, the die was cast.

Given the Railway Inspectorate's proud history of seeking to extirpate all elements of chance from the safe operation of the railways over the previous 120 years, it seems astonishing that they should have introduced new equipment which under foreseeable, and therefore *predictable*, circumstances, produced situations where, whether or not a collision occurred, was, to all intents and purposes, in the lap of the gods. One expert witness to the Hixon Inquiry, Colin Buchanan, Professor of Transport at Imperial College, said:

> my impression has been that the [Railways] Board accepted the drastic departure from railway practice which is involved in half-barrier crossings, on the assumption that in any collision it would be the road vehicle that would suffer, not the train. This assumption has been falsified [by the Hixon accident] and the spectre of horrific damage to a train has been introduced.

It is worth noting here that Buchanan does not distinguish between British Railways and the Railway Inspectorate, and to a non-rail industry insider, even one as able and experienced as Buchanan, the distinction would not have seemed important. In point of fact, the Inspectorate were acting as zealots, who were convinced of the efficacy and superiority of AHB crossings and were determined to impose them onto the rail network regardless of any reservations others might have. Professor Buchanan also brought up the possibility of a motor-bus or coach becoming immobilized on a crossing, which, given the similar length and low ground clearance, seemed to fit into the same risk category as an articulated lorry, although obviously such a vehicle would probably not have quite the same 'train killing' capacity. Rather, it was the thought of a bus or coach full of people, and the effect of an express train impacting on it, that had caused the good professor to shudder.

We shall hear more from Buchanan later, when his recommendations as to the best way forward for automatic level-crossings formed the basis of the

Inquiry's findings on this important matter; his highlighting of the particular hazard of a slow-moving or stationary vehicle, of a sufficient size to inflict serious damage on a train, presented a circumstance which, as became apparent from the evidence of Colonel McMullen and Mr Scott-Malden, the Railway Inspectorate claimed not to have foreseen at all.

Although the oversight of the actual installation of AHB crossings in Britain was clearly with first Colonel McMullen and then from November 1961 onwards Colonel Reed, responsibility for associated matters, such as the provision of publicity about the new crossings, is not so easy to attribute. There was a committee of the Ministry of Transport in existence, under the chairmanship of Mr Frank Bickerton, its Chief Information Officer; this committee was charged with planning and executing publicity campaigns in association with the Policy Divisions concerned. Mr Bickerton told the Hixon Inquiry that in June 1963 the Railway Inspectorate had informed him that 'it would be necessary to consider how publicity should be given to ... this type of level-crossing ... so that they would be understood and accepted', and in October of the same year the Inspectorate emphasized that there 'was a need for adequate publicity measures before automatic half- barriers were brought into operation'. In particular, at meetings of Bickerton's committee, reference was made by Colonel Reed to the publicity measures employed by the Netherlands State Railways, when they had introduced AHB crossings in the 1950s: a short film entitled *Thirty seconds, or Eternity* had been produced, which, as its name implies, emphasized the existential danger posed if a road user did not wait behind the half-barrier. This film was shown to saturation point in every cinema across the Netherlands, both before, during and after the Dutch crossing automation programme was carried out. Deliberately and blatantly, leaving little room for misunderstanding, the message was hammered home to the correct target audience: adult motorists.

The aim was to make the Dutch vehicle-driving population aware of the new hazard that was being put amongst them, and the necessary procedure for safely dealing with it. As well as the film, a series of leaflets were produced for distribution to all households in the general vicinity of one of the new crossings, which were clearly designed to instil some frisson of dread in the reader, the text of one translates as, 'Red is the colour of blood, it is also the colour of the lights on the level-crossing'. This superimposed on a suitably gory hand print.

It is to Colonel Reed's credit that he saw the merit in this approach; somebody in the administration of the Netherlands State Railways had recognized the vital importance of getting across the message of how potentially dangerous the new crossings were if not treated with due caution. However, although Reed was in overall charge of the physical installation of each AHB crossing, he was not in charge of the provision of necessary publicity to the general public. As outlined above, that was the ultimate responsibility of Mr Bickerton's committee. By 1964 there had been only twenty-four AHB crossings installed in Britain, and the decision was made at this point, just prior to a rapid increase in the rate of crossing installation (by December 1967 there were 198 AHB crossings) to concentrate on locally focused publicity for each new crossing, which was to consist of leaflets distributed to schools in the vicinity of each AHB crossing, together with wall charts for each school. Small numbers of the leaflets were sent out to the Police Authority in each area where the automated crossings were to be installed, presumably so they could be displayed in police stations, for any interested police officers, or those members of the public who happened upon them, to peruse. As well as this direct provision of information by British Railways, they also agreed to contact local newspapers with details of the new crossings, in the hope that this would generate an article or two; and that, pretty much, was that.

The Dutch approach, commended to them by Colonel Reed, had been discussed by Bickerton's committee in 1964, which at that time, concluded that 'National publicity ... must be considered from the viewpoints of desirability and practicability'. Furthermore, Bickerton, in his role as chairman, then expressed reservations 'as to its desirability, as too much National Publicity would invite general emotional reactions and a possible feeling of danger attached to the crossings'. This last phrase is underlined in blue in the archive copy, with an exclamation mark in the margin, possibly the work of the Hixon Inquiry Chairman Brian Gibbens, who may have been wondering just how many times 'pennies did not drop' in the story of the installation of automatic crossings in this country. After all, an appropriate sense of the potential danger of the new crossings, was precisely what the Ministry of Transport should have been seeking to transmit to the British public, just as their Dutch counterparts had done with *Thirty seconds, or Eternity*. One gets an overwhelming sense of the 'committee process' pushing towards an acceptable compromise solution as far as publicity for AHB crossings was concerned; by late 1966 a television 'short' about automatic level-crossing introduction had been produced and broadcast a hundred times that year, but it was discontinued, and nothing similar was provided during 1967. In short, just as the countrywide AHB crossing installation programme was gathering pace, there was virtually nothing in the way of national publicity being provided. Of course, one man in particular, Colonel Reed, was in a position to have insisted that a proper attempt was made to educate adult motorists as to the reality of things at the new crossings; and we know that Reed succeeded at a meeting of Bickerton's committee in 1963 in getting the initial TV 'short' made and approved for countrywide broadcasting on British television. However, the need for the publicity to be long term and ubiquitous was lost within the committee process. Just as more AHB crossings were being installed, Reed was unsuccessful in his attempt to achieve national publicity for the new automatic crossings, at the time that it was most needed. There is no need to deploy any hindsight in coming to judgement as to his subsequent actions; Reed appreciated the necessity of adequate publicity for the new crossings, at the time. However, he chose to press ahead with the programme of AHB crossing installation, presumably falling back on the view that once the public had experienced the new crossings, once or twice, they would be 'educated'. It is difficult not to agree with Professor Colin Buchanan that the possibility of an accident arising from a completely naïve driver encountering an AHB crossing for the first time *did* occur to those promulgating their introduction, but that they also believed that any accidents, whilst regrettable, would be few and that the resultant publicity would rapidly complete the job of informing road users that they should treat the new crossings with respect. It is worth reading the preceding sentence through a couple of times, because it is only when the situation is laid out in such stark terms that it becomes apparent just how much of a hazard the Railway Inspectorate was introducing on to Britain's railway system. What lay behind this willingness to countenance what, on the face of it, was a reckless departure from the Railway Inspectorate's renowned emphasis on making railway operations as safe as possible? Part of the answer certainly lies in Colonel Reed's determination to push on with the automation programme; it had become his 'baby' and he was clearly of the view that any increased risk of accidents at level-crossings as a result of the advent of AHB protection was a risk worth taking, and moreover was more than balanced out by the advantages that the new equipment would bring in terms of improved traffic flow on the road network as a whole. Encouraging this viewpoint was the apparent weight of statistical evidence relating to general accidents and fatalities on British roads compared to the same at level-crossings; putting it bluntly, in the early 1960s it was a very bad year indeed when the ratio of general road deaths to level-crossing fatalities was less than 2,000 to one. Reed knew that the old gated crossings were really very safe, far safer than the road network in general at any rate, and he could see no reason why the new AHB crossings would not be just as safe, once the vehicle driving public had got used to them, which would, of course, only take one or two individual encounters for each motorist. In a limited sense he was right, but a considerable danger lay within the only very gradually diminishing population, in the statistical sense of that word, who still retained the idea that 'the Railway' would not allow them on to the crossing if there was a train coming. This belief was not at all inconsistent with being aware of the new crossings' existence.

The other reason why Reed was willing to introduce a level-crossing operating system which was so radically different to the old system, was a failure to appreciate the difference between the high levels of control that existed over what were purely railway operations, with the old gated crossings and the potentially zero levels of control that would exist, once it was down to individual vehicle drivers as to whether they should proceed onto the railway tracks in front of them. Reed, and those others involved in the theoretical planning behind the AHB crossings assumed that virtually the totality of vehicle drivers would act rationally and obey the relatively straightforward requirement to halt at the descended half-barrier, and then move their vehicles *briskly* across the railway lines when it was indicated it was safe to do so. The reasoning was, that in the early days of AHB crossing introduction, there might be a small number of accidents involving drivers totally unaware of the new dispensation but that, as Professor Colin Buchanan put his finger on, these accidents would not seriously inconvenience the Railway. What was not envisaged by those introducing AHB crossings was a naïve driver in charge of a vehicle capable of wrecking a train, if it was obstructing a crossing. Or at least, that was what both Colonel McMullen, the Chief Inspector of Railways, and Mr Scott-Malden, Under-Secretary for the Railways Group at the Ministry of Transport, maintained under sceptical questioning by Chairman Gibbens, of the Hixon Inquiry, when giving their evidence. Also, the Railway Inspectorate were conscious that the new non-signal protected AHB crossings, would deliver increased capacity on the lines and thereby the 'glittering prize' of increased average speed of trains. That was the key 'railwayman's ' reason why they were pressing ahead with the conversions.

The minutes of meetings of Bickerton's publicity and information committee shows that Colonel Reed, having made a couple of attempts to achieve something similar to the Netherlands Railways' approach to making the public aware of the new crossings, effectively gave up and concentrated on getting as many of the new crossings installed as quickly as possible; 1967 saw the number of AHB crossings increase to 198, eighteen of them with no permanent telephones for the use of the general public, in the barrier posts, or adjacent to them. Colonel Reed had of course ensured that the standard model of AHB crossing was to have no telephones for the use of the public, by altering the enabling legislation first in 1963 and again in 1966. Quite what one unforeseen effect was, of Reed wanting automatic crossings installed without telephones, is a matter which penetrates to the heart of the causation of the Hixon disaster; because he did not want telephones for most future crossings, he paid scant regard to the design and placement of signage for those telephones, except that he imposed, in April 1964, what he considered to be an ideal, 'killing two birds with one stone' signboard on British Railways, which read:

IN EMERGENCY
or before crossing with exceptional
or heavy loads or cattle
PHONE SIGNALMAN

The lettering was in black, on a white painted metal signboard measuring 30½ inches wide by 14 inches tall and the signboard was to be erected approximately seven feet off the ground on top of a metal post. The idea was that the words 'IN EMERGENCY – PHONE SIGNALMAN' could be read quickly, if you were in an emergency situation say, and if you weren't, then you would clearly have time to read the enclosed lower case message. What could be simpler or more obvious? Reed, under cross-examination at the Hixon Inquiry, stuck to this viewpoint, even though it was pointed out to him that the lower-case message was the one that would need to be read first by somebody approaching the crossing, with an exceptional or heavy load, if they were going to be able to act upon it.

Although there was a tremendous amount of investment in innovatory technology as regards the new crossings, those taking the policy decisions thought that they were already 'proved safe', both from their use in other countries and from their early 'experimental use' in a few quiet locations mainly in the South and East of England. This possibly explains why only a desultory attempt was made to inform and educate the public as to the correct procedures to be followed, if one found oneself confronted by one of these revolutionary new crossings; two short paragraphs (57 and 58) had been included in the Ministry of Transport's *Highway Code* 1959 edition (amended 1961), dealing with Railway level-crossings and explaining that automatic level-crossings were to be introduced into Britain. Here they are in full:

Railway level crossings

57.   At railway level crossings without gates slow down, look both ways, listen and make sure it is safe before crossing the lines. At crossings with gates but no gatekeeper, open *both* gates before starting to cross and do not stop your vehicle on the lines. Close the gates after you.

58.   Some level crossings are being equipped with the Continental type of short barrier, which only covers half the width of the road and is worked automatically by approaching trains. The barriers are timed to fall *just before a train reaches the crossing*. Red flashing signals and gongs will be provided, and they will operate before the barriers begin to fall, in order to warn traffic. Do not pass the signals when they are flashing, and do not zigzag round the barriers.

Never cross before the barriers are lifted; there may be a second train coming.

BE PATIENT – NEVER ZIGZAG

In addition there was a small, annotated, line drawing of what one of the new 'Continental type' crossings might look like, located twelve pages further on from the two paragraphs. (As can be seen from plate 27, the diagram looks more like a border-control checkpoint than a level-crossing.) This was the only written material that was to be provided to the general public, nationwide, on the subject of automated level-crossings, up until the publication of a new edition of the *Code* in 1969, after the *Hixon Inquiry Report* had given its recommendations (not surprisingly, the new edition had three full pages of advice on dealing with the automatic crossings).

Although the two paragraphs are supposed to provide information about railway level-crossings, of course they give no information about what were still the most numerous type of level-crossing that motorists would encounter, that is, fully gated and manned crossings. This was not because the authors of the *Code* considered that enough was already known about these, but because legally it would have been judged most unwise to comment on how motorists should deal with crossings, where the legal responsibility for their safe use by vehicles remained in the hands of British Railways. The ham-fisted, yet at the same time, underhand nature of the AHB crossing introduction programme is brilliantly illustrated by these two short paragraphs, in that they don't make any mention of the fact that at the new 'Continental type' crossings the full, legal responsibility for getting safely across the railway lines now lay with the motorist. This is not a pernickety criticism of an oversight, because the 1959 edition of the *Code* links most of its ninety-four paragraphs to the actual statutes that give them authority, in a section entitled 'The Law Demands'. But not paragraphs 57 and 58. Surely, the most fundamental shift in the law regarding responsibility for safety at level-crossings for 120 years, should have been clearly spelled out and its actual legal basis in Section 66 of the 1957 British Transport Commission Act, identified? If it had been, then some more people would have realized that the situation at the new crossings was very different to that which they were used to. Including of course, the Road Haulage Association, the RAC and the AA.

No, not an oversight, a choice was made by those in the Railway Inspectorate and the Ministry of Transport generally, overseeing the AHB programme, to keep this information out of the one place it would have been seen by the greatest number of drivers. Best not to alarm people unnecessarily! There is also one almost comical observation to be drawn from paragraphs 57 and 58, and it concerns the instructions as to what to do if confronted with a crossing 'without gates': a motorist was to 'slow down, look both ways, listen and make sure it is safe before crossing the lines'. Now, it might be a coincidence, but nonplussed railwaymen during the early days of AHB crossing introduction reported many instances of motorists slowing down when approaching the new crossings, even with the barriers raised, and then looking both ways, up and down the lines before proceeding gingerly over the crossing. After all, the new crossings were *without gates* and many conscientious motorists who knew their *Highway Code*, would have considered they were doing the right thing by following the instructions in paragraph 57. Of course, they were acting in precisely the opposite way to that which they should have been behaving, that is, moving briskly across an open AHB crossing. This was what those in charge of the crossing automation programme wanted motorists to do, but the only widely available written advice told them to do the exact reverse of this. As with so much else connected with AHB crossing introduction, this kind of detail had never been thought through. And, as we know only too well, the devil is always in the detail.

Moreover, in the two 1959 *Highway Code* paragraphs there is no reference to any telephone procedure, either in the event of an emergency, or if a heavy or slow-moving load was to be taken over a crossing. This omission can only be easily understood if one accepts that initially in the late 1950s, before any of the new crossings were installed in this country, whether telephones for the use of the public were to be provided had not been definitively decided upon. They were thought by some of those closely involved in the installation process to be unnecessary; some foreign railway systems operated AHB crossings without telephones and there was a school of thought which argued that telephones were likely to interfere with the timely operation of the new automatic crossings. It is this conflict between safety and the perceived importance of the convenience and timeousness of traffic movements, both road and rail, that underlies the apparent reluctance to install telephones at the new crossings, and which certainly crystallized decisively in the mind of Colonel Reed, to the extent that he was attempting to install AHB crossings with no telephones, right up until the last possible moment in September 1966.

Although it is impossible to say with any certainty, it is fair to assume that Reed, having failed to convince Bickerton and his committee of the need for a national AHB crossing publicity campaign, did his best to promote awareness of the coming of the new crossings, through arranging some coverage for distribution via newsreels in cinemas nationwide. British Movietone News cameras were invited along when, on 22 June 1964, a demonstration was provided for the press in the goods yard at Marylebone station, and the newsreel film still exists of the proceedings; the mock-up is of a single track crossing with just the one half-barrier. First an articulated parcels lorry crosses and then an unusual-looking, short and squat, 'heavy haulage' tractor-type vehicle, carrying a bulk liquids tank bolted awkwardly along its side, is sent smartly across just before the barrier comes down. So, clearly somebody at the Railway Inspectorate or British Railways, thought that it was a good idea to show the press large and unwieldy vehicles successfully and safely negotiating one of the new crossings. The train that triggers the barriers to fall is a two-carriage diesel multiple unit, travelling at an appropriately sedate speed for a goods yard, no more than 20 mph, and certainly not the specified 90 mph of a mainline express. Waiting obediently beside the road vehicles are a selection of pedestrians, including a mother with a toddler and a group of schoolboys in short trousers. Also clearly visible towards the end of the clip, in amongst a scrum of officials and reporters, are Colonel Reed and the most senior member of the Railway Inspectorate, Colonel McMullen. Both men are in 'mufti issue' belted cream mackintoshes and black bowler hats, the bulky Reed towering over the diminutive McMullen, like badly out of kilter Thompson Twins. (Curiously, although I have found plenty of photographs of his four contemporaries in the Inspectorate, I have been unable to locate any other identified image of Colonel Reed.) What is noticeably absent from the Marylebone mock-up is a telephone, or any notice issuing instructions as to how to proceed. Presumably, it had been decided that as this was a public relations demonstration, there was no need to intrude too much in the way of reality as to what the public might actually encounter at an AHB-equipped crossing. Of course, at this stage, in June of 1964, the question as to whether they should have telephones for the use of the general public in the event of an emergency, was, as has been discussed, still a moot point, in particular in the considerations of the one man, Colonel Reed, who was, to use a modern phrase, 'driving' the installation of automatic crossings onto the railway network.

As I have stated, my father's role in preventing a catastrophic accident at Leominster was not mentioned at all in the *Hixon Inquiry Report*, although it is unquestionably the same incident that is described in paragraph 109:

On that date [8 November 1966] Mr James Howard Horton, who is employed by Robert Wynn and Sons Limited as a driver, drove a Scammell low-loader lorry, carrying a crane weighing more than 15 tons, over the recently installed automatic crossing at Leominster. At that time the road surface had not been finally made up, and there was a small ramp of about 4 inches' drop on the further side of the crossing. Mr Horton drove over at about 5 miles per hour but, as the front of his tractor went down the ramp, the low-loader grounded and he could not move. A railwayman (believed to be a signalman) from the station nearby called out, 'You can't park there,' to which Mr Horton replied, 'Park, indeed! I am grounded on the crossing.' The signalman then informed him that there was a train due and that, once the lights began to flash, it would mean that the train was only a matter of seconds up the line. On that stretch of line the maximum speed was 90 miles per hour and, obviously this was a grave emergency. Mr Horton told the signalman, 'You had better get on the 'phone and stop the train as I am going to be here for perhaps an hour jacking this lot up to get it off the crossing,' but apparently, the signalman was unable to do so because the train was already too close. Mr Horton then, with great courage, got into his driving seat and, by violently accelerating the engine and letting the clutch in, caused the front end of the vehicle to leap into the air, and thus to drag it clear from the rail, just as the express whizzed behind him.

So clearly, according to this, the only person who took any positive action to forestall the impending collision, was the lorry driver, Horton. Furthermore, in paragraph 110, the direct consequences of the near-miss are focused almost entirely on the actions of Horton:

> After the train had gone, a telecommunication and signals officer of the Railways came over and, in the course of conversation, told Mr Horton that this was a new automatic crossing and that the time element was about 30 seconds before the approach of a train. Mr Horton thought this was a ridiculously short time to expect a vehicle such as his to clear the line; he thought one would not even have time to push a stalled car off. So he reported the matter to his employers, Robert Wynn and Sons Limited.

This left me with a number of questions hanging in the air, as it were: besides the obvious one regarding my father's actions being erased from the record, there was also a tantalizing question as to what had happened to the train; if it had been slowing when it ran over the crossing, then at some point it would have halted, which tended to confirm my father's version as the reality, and indeed, a letter written by Wynns to British Rail on 19 November 1966, advising them of what had occurred on the 8th, contains the following: 'We believe that the express stopped at some half mile beyond the crossing. Our driver reported the incident to railway officials at Leominster, also to the civil police.' (The train was in fact pulled up in Leominster station, about half a mile distant from the crossing). However, in their response to this letter, British Railways in the person of a Mr H. M. Lattimer, Assistant General Manager of the Western Region, state: 'A train travelling at high speed with no warning of anything amiss ahead takes something like three-quarters of a mile to stop, and this would explain why there was no means of stopping the express in question before it reached the crossing. *It had evidently already passed any warning signal that could have been given to it.*' (my emphasis). So, British Railways' considered response was that there was no attempt made to halt or slow the train (and no mention is made of exactly what speed it was travelling at as it came through, although it is implied it was 'travelling at high speed').

Lattimer's letter was dated 29 November 1966, a full three weeks after the incident, and therefore allowing plenty of time for internal enquiries to have been made of the five railway staff, including an S&T Inspector, present at Leominster on the day, not to mention the signalman in the Leominster South End box, or even the train driver. It only takes a moment's thought for anyone familiar with the necessarily meticulous, written record-keeping of the Railway at that time, particularly in signal-boxes, to realize that either no serious attempt had been made by British Railways' local senior management to establish precisely what had occurred, *or* enquiries had indeed taken place, and the result was the carefully phrased obfuscation of Lattimer's letter. The *Hixon Inquiry Report* is scathing of the 'famous' letter, as Mr Gibbens the chairman ironically describes it, paragraph 114 of the report saying this:

> That letter was remarkable for its arrogance and lack of insight (on a par with the statement 'You can't park there') at a high executive level in British Railways, and it is most unfortunate that the writer did not point out the hazard to slowly moving vehicles and the requirement that the driver of any heavy or exceptional load must telephone the signalman before crossing, which was a precaution vital to the safety of automatic crossings. Had he done so, we can only speculate as to whether the accident at Hixon a year later would have happened: in all probability it would not.

Having made this very profound and penetrating comment about the tragic consequences of not mentioning the telephone procedure, the Chairman of the Inquiry, who was also of course the author of the report, perhaps surprisingly, does not then pursue the matter as to *why* no mention was made of telephone procedure; rather it is put down to 'arrogance and lack of insight', and a comedic parallel is drawn between the lamentable communication skills of railwaymen, both high and lowly. Even though he refers to it, disparagingly, as the 'famous' letter, Chairman Gibbens takes it at face value, and not having called its author before his inquiry as a witness to question, unfortunately, that was the only option open to him. Here is Lattimer's letter to Wynns in full, just as it was reproduced in the *Hixon Inquiry Report*:

> Mr Banwell has passed forward your letter of the 19th November for my attention. I am naturally as much concerned as you are about this incident, which might have had much more serious consequences.
>
> Automatic level-crossing barriers have been installed at a number of points on British Railways and are, of course, widespread in other countries. There is no difference at Leominster from any other barrier crossing . The design is approved by the Ministry of Transport, both on the railway and on the road side, and the contingency of a road vehicle stalling on the level-crossing and becoming immovable was one that was considered and found too remote to be taken as a serious consequence.
>
> Apart from barrier operated crossings, we have several hundred occupation and accommodation crossings on the above line, mainly for agricultural use and similar conditions apply there should the occupier attempt to use the crossing for a complicated or heavy machine. In brief, road vehicles must not become immobile on these crossings. If they do, they not only become a hazard to themselves, but they have become a hazard to trains and to whomever are travelling in them. I think I am quoting

correctly what would be the view of the Ministry Inspecting Officer of Railways. Had there been a serious accident, it would have been subject to a Ministry Inquiry and the principal point of the Inquiry would not have been the safety of the crossing, which is an approved one, but why the vehicle was on the line when the train approached, and the barriers were about to close to road traffic.

The time interval between the warning lights and the closing of the barriers has been especially laid down by the minister, and again, there is no difference at Leominster than at other crossings. If the warning is too long the public become accustomed to the length of time and start taking unjustifiable risks to beat the lights.

A train travelling at high speed with no warning of anything amiss takes something like three-quarters of a mile to stop, and this would explain why there was no means of stopping the express in question before it reached the crossing. It had evidently already passed any warning signal that could have been given to it.

Nothing which has been said above detracts in any way from the action of your driver, which appears to have been in every way commendable. We are obviously grateful that he removed the hazard to safety at a risk to himself. I must emphasize, however, that the hazard was of your firm's making and it is fortunate it was not more than a hazard.

Once the flashing lights start, then road vehicles are in a position of having to stop because of 'major road ahead'. I would ask you to consider whether the same hazard would have been created if your vehicle had been coming out of a difficult side road onto a main trunk road with high speed vehicles on it and had stalled across the main road. However, I am passing on this correspondence to the local Divisional Manager so that he can satisfy himself that there was no fault on the railway side that in any way contributed to the incident and that our staff did all that could be expected of them in the circumstances.

The letter is rather a stunner at first glance, particularly if it is being read in retrospect, as it is presented by Chairman Gibbens in the *Hixon Inquiry Report*, as a bizarrely incompetent response to Wynns' justified concerns. However, it is possible to place it back in late November of 1966, as a robust statement of British Railways' position concerning AHB crossings; in particular there is Lattimer's implication that Wynns' lorry was merely 'stalled' on the crossing, not stuck on an obstruction; that is, he was questioning the veracity of Wynns' driver's version of events at Leominster. It is worth noting that this challenging of whether the lorry was actually stuck, also formed part of the cross-examination of James Horton, Wynns' driver at Leominster, during the Hixon Inquiry; indeed, British Railways brought forward technical evidence stating that it was impossible for Wynns' low-loader to have jammed where it did! The line of argument, as it was developed in the first week of the inquiry hearings, was that Horton, the lorry driver, had deliberately brought his vehicle to a halt astride the crossing, whether from reckless bravado, or through a mistaken belief that there would be plenty of time to 'get on the phone and stop the trains'. (This was during the careful, but ultimately unsuccessful, legal assault on Wynns by the Ministry of Transport barristers, during the Hixon Inquiry. If things had turned out differently, then Lattimer's letter might not have been dismissed as merely arrogant or lacking in insight.)

Also, after a couple of readings of the letter, what comes through is that Lattimer is firmly putting the responsibility for the introduction of the new crossings and also their safe operation onto the Railway Inspectorate and Ministry of Transport. Rather than judging Lattimer as merely exhibiting 'arrogance and a lack of insight', if Gibbens had had access to the correspondence relating to yet another near-miss at Leominster level-crossing, between the Railway Inspectorate and Lattimer (the so-called Colonel Gower incident that took place on Sunday, 4 December 1966) then he would have seen straight away that Lattimer was trying, without risking his own position of course, to distance British Railways from the Inspectorate as far as automatic level-crossings were concerned. Like the members of the Inspectorate, Lattimer was also a former Royal Engineer officer, having reached the rank of acting Major during the Second World War and, moreover, he had only quite recently arrived as an Assistant General Manager of Western Region, having previously been a movements manager on the Eastern Region, the early testing location for AHB crossings.

What he thought about the new crossings can probably best be judged from the fact that he always identified them very closely with the Railway Inspectorate in all his correspondence on the matter. Instead of assuming arrogance on Lattimer's part, Gibbens should have been asking whether his referral of the matter to his divisional managers had any outcome, which of course it did, in that one of them went on to inform Colonel Reed, in person, in late February 1967 of what had happened at Leominster on 8 November, 1966. The problem was, that although Gibbens was a highly intelligent man, this was his first attempt at investigating a case involving railway procedure and he thereby overlooked some clues that would have given him a far more accurate picture of what was happening, as far as installation of AHB crossings was concerned. In particular, he completely failed to pick up on the 'turf war' that was going on regarding the provision of telephones at the crossings, between the Railway Inspectorate and British Railways' national management, particularly the S&T Department. Lattimer, as a regional manager, would have found himself stuck between the two warring sides.

The fact that Lattimer did not mention the use of a telephone in his letter to Wynns can be easily explained, because at the time of the incident, he believed that no phones for the use of the general public in an emergency were in place at the Leominster level-crossing. Crucially, he also knew that at some of the most recently installed crossings up and down the country, there were no phones of any kind provided. So literally, Lattimer could not have advised Wynns in general terms as to necessary telephone procedure at level-crossings, because not all of the crossings their lorry drivers might encounter were equipped with phones!

Chapter 4

'Well the lorry driver and his mate took off in high dudgeon, and we went home'

The National Archive at Kew, has amongst its collections, extensive records of the day-to-day proceedings of British Railways and its interactions with Her Majesty's Government, in particular, the Ministry of Transport; it also stores the full case papers and evidence bundles for the Hixon Inquiry itself, in some seventeen, separate, substantial manila files, which have been available for public viewing since 1999, when they were released from the standard thirty-year embargo. Most of the files consist of the forty-two days' worth of transcript of the proceedings of the Inquiry, however two or three are the bundles of witness 'proofs' (statements), letters, plans, photographs and other documents examined during the Inquiry.

One file in particular consists of documents emanating from various places and times, but all relating to the Leominster automatic crossing, and, which taken together, clearly delineate the real situation there on 8 November 1966. Many of the document pages have red and blue pencil underlinings, circlings and linking arrows on them, and I initially thought that these were the work of Brian Gibbens, the Chairman of the Inquiry, drawing together the threads of evidence, which enabled him to establish the facts. However, I am now of the opinion that the contents of this file and the various investigative markings are just as likely to be the result of Colonel Reed's review of the evidence as to goings on at Leominster, which he carried out, at speed, in early March 1968. Certainly, some of the documents never came publicly before the Hixon Inquiry. The key document (which also confirms my father's version of events) is the witness statement of Leslie Lloyd, the Movements Manager of British Railways Western Region, at the time of the inquiry, although not at the time of the Leominster incident. In it Lloyd states:

At the crossing at the time of the incident of 8th November, 1966 there were, so far as the Board are concerned, five men present. They were Signalman Blower who was acting as attendant and four men from the Signal and Telecommunications Department – Inspector Hallett (to whom Mr Horton spoke), Technicians A. Jones, P. Jones and I. [sic] Westwood. Westwood telephoned Leominster Signal Box from the barrier telephone as soon as he saw that the Scammell had stopped on the crossing because he knew that a down passenger express was due. While he was telephoning, the lights began to flash and the bells to ring. The signalman at Leominster immediately reversed his down Distant signal and from the fact that the train was braking as it went over the crossing, it is thought that the driver saw the change of aspect of the signal: alternatively he may have seen the vehicle.

There you have it then: my father's story is confirmed in all its essentials; however, three details differ: firstly, the telephone used to make the call was not in the barrier housing; it was in fact a permanent phone provided for the use of farmers, fixed onto the warning lights mast on the Ludlow side of the crossing. There were no barrier phones in place on the day of the near-collision; if my father had had to connect a 'plug-in' railway handset into one of the barrier housings, this would have increased the time taken to make the phone call; given that the express missed the back of the transporter by only a few inches, using a 'plug-in' handset would probably have spelled disaster. Moreover, in those circumstances, it would have been suicidally dangerous for anyone making such a call from a barrier housing.

The second differing detail is that Lloyd suggests that the train driver may have seen the lorry on the crossing, and braked as a result of this, rather than reacting to the signals. Don't forget, it was around 5.30 p.m. on a winter evening, the sun had set an hour before, so visibility would have been limited, and to all intents and purposes it would have been fully dark (*see* plate 23). What Lloyd fails to take account of as well, is that train crew had been instructed not to brake: if from a distance of a few hundred yards out they saw traffic on the new automatic crossings, *they were to keep going*, on the basis that the crossing would be clear by the time their train ran on to it. The third difference relates to which signal the driver of the oncoming train reacted to; Lloyd specifies the Distant signal, which was approximately 900 yards out from the crossing, just in front of the mechanisms that activated the barriers. My father said the express had already passed the Distant before it was switched, and therefore its driver reacted to the Home signal which was just 300 yards away from the crossing. All three of these differing details tend to reduce the importance of my father's phone call, deliberately so in my opinion. Because of course, by suggesting that his actions may have been superfluous, Lloyd plays down the seriousness of the situation and echoes S&T Inspector Hallett's original response to Horton the lorry driver on 8 November 1966; although there may have been a close shave, as it were, the new automatic system at Leominster crossing would have functioned as it was intended to do. If, on the other hand, a catastrophic accident had only been narrowly averted by the irregular use of signals, *that were never intended to form any part of the new system*, then that would have been a much more troubling matter.

(Lloyd's letter was also to prove potentially devastating to the situation of the Railway Inspectorate, in particular that of Colonel Reed, because Lloyd states that Reed was made fully aware of the incident at Leominster of 8 November 1966, at the final inspection meeting held at the crossing on 23 February 1967. Reed denied he had ever spoken to railway officials about the incident. Quite why this apparently compelling line of inquiry, which was toyed with by both the British Railways' legal team, and to some extent Chairman Gibbens himself during the inquiry, but was never really pursued to its conclusion, remains for me one of the most puzzling and disturbing aspects of the whole Hixon affair.)

On a personal level, Lloyd's letter also provided information that offered a slim chance of verifying my father's story directly; the names of his workmates were specified: 'A. Jones' was Arthur Jones from Ludlow, 'P. Jones' was Phil Jones, also from Ludlow. I remembered both men from my childhood, Arthur was the senior technician and a few years older than my father. Phil was younger, a tank crew veteran of the Korean War, who had played guitar at my sister's wedding in 1970. I decided to try to contact him, as I reasoned he stood most chance of still being alive. Having looked up all the likely Jones' phone numbers in Ludlow, I tried the first on the list, and Bingo!, it was Phil. He was now 82 and living alone in his house in Ludlow; he told me that Arthur had died some years earlier, as had Inspector Hallett and Austen Blower, the crossing attendant. This left Phil as the last railway witness of the events at Leominster crossing. He remembered the incident well and agreed to meet me at the crossing, to talk things through on the spot, which we did the following week. Phil had not altered much to my way of thinking since I had last seen him some thirty years before: still the same wispy grey hair (although a little less of it) and trusty briar pipe. He pointed out where their small, 'BR Yellow' Commer van had been parked up, twenty or so yards away from the crossing, on the Leominster side. He also indicated where the 'home' signal had been positioned, some 300 yards north of us on the Down side of the tracks, and described how the grounded Scammell's trailer and its load had completely obstructed the crossing.

Although many things have changed at Leominster crossing in the years since 1966, one thing is unaltered, and that is the dimensions and orientation of the crossing in regard to both the railway and the roadway: the front of the trailer, jamming as it did on the Leominster side of the crossing, would have left both railway tracks solidly blocked, with the mobile crane on its back, squarely in between the Up and the Down lines, with the jib of the crane stretching back to the road on the Ludlow side of the crossing. The Scammell tractor unit was clear, just, on the Leominster side, pulled up next to a house which is still there. On the other side of the road in 1966, was the obsolete Kington junction signal-box (since demolished), which was being used as an observation platform whilst the AHB crossing conversion work was taking place. Astonishingly, the box had no telephone link with the Railway network, nor even an ordinary

GPO telephone, so what precisely the railwayman manning it was supposed to do in the event of an emergency is anyone's guess. In actual fact its use as an observation platform and the presence of a 'signalman' was worse than useless, because this gave out a false message that something *could* be done, which of course was precisely what Horton, the lorry driver, thought the situation to be, hence his request that someone 'get on the phone'.

(Contemporary film footage shows that the steps up to the signal-box were parallel to the railway tracks and quite shallow, with a small landing outside the door, ideal for the signalman to come out and stand on, which proved to be very fortunate on Sunday, 4 December 1966, a few weeks after the Scammell grounding, when yet another fatal incident was narrowly averted at Leominster crossing; as will be explored in the next chapter, with the story of Lieutenant-Colonel Gower, Commandant of the Army Apprentices College at Chepstow, who together with his wife had an extremely narrow and alarming escape from violent death.)

Having appreciated just how restricted a space the drama had been played out in, I asked Phil to recount what he remembered, as it came back to him:

It was a real brown-trouser job, the train was slowing as it came through, with sparks coming off of the wheels, and right up until the last second it looked like it was going to hit. The train driver pulled up in Leominster station and refused to take it on any further, he was that shook up. He stayed the night in Leominster, and they had to get a relief driver from the Depot at Hereford to take the train on. It was a big heavy diesel loco, with seven or eight coaches on.

(The locomotive was a Class 37, weighing 112 tons and brought into service in the early 1960s; remarkably, over fifty years later, some are still in service on the rail network.)

How long had the whole incident lasted?

It was only about three or four minutes total, from when the Scammell grounded and the driver got out and said, "Call this a fucking *level-crossing?*" We were all on the Leominster side of the crossing, about twenty yards clear, next to the van, and were just on the point of going home. Mr Hallett went to speak to the driver, and Jack nipped across to the phone on the warning lights mast over on the other side, and called Leominster South End box to see if they could change the signal. Around about this time Austen Blower came out onto the steps of his box and shouted to the driver, "You can't park that there, mate!" When the barriers came down I yelled across to your dad to get clear, and the rest of us moved back sharpish, although old Austen was still on the steps. Anyway, the driver had got back into his cab and managed to shift it just in time. He was not a happy man after it was all over, and young Hallett had a bit of a job calming him down. There was actually another extra chap with us, Eddie Williams from Craven Arms, as far as I can remember, because putting in these new crossings was such a rush job. The chief S&T Inspector, 'Flash' Williams – he was known as 'Flash' because he expected things to be done in a flash – was badgering us to get the work completed. Don't forget that the signal that was altered, the one that saved the day, had nothing at all to do with controlling the crossing mechanism: it was just meant to protect Leominster station track section. Your dad was the one who realized that it was the only chance that was left.

I asked Phil if he could recall what occurred afterwards: 'Well, the lorry driver and his mate took off in high dudgeon, and we went home. There was nothing else to be done: the train driver had made his phone call from Leominster station, and left the train, and that was that.' Phil's considered view on the matter was this:

You see, we didn't like these new AHB crossings much, because they weren't linked in to any signals of their own; don't forget that if something like this had happened say at Bromfield crossing [just north of Ludlow] which we converted at around about the same time, then nothing could have been done, because there were no track section signals there at all.

Even though nearly five decades had gone by, Phil was still moved to fury by the affront to safe railway working practices that the AHB crossing installation process had entailed, in particular the removal of the previously existing telephone in the Kington junction signal-box, 'It was stripped out … just a shell … what was the point in that? All the so-called 'attendant' could do was wave his arms and shout.'

Curiously, there exists film of a diesel locomotive approaching Leominster crossing from the direction of Ludlow (B&R Video productions, Volume 99: *Herefordshire Byways*) that was shot from the drivers cab and was taken in the spring of 1964, long before the conversion to AHB working, and clearly shows the old solid wooden crossing gates. This train is travelling at just over 40 mph, as can be quite quickly calculated from the four seconds it takes it to cover the space between the old Kington junction points and the crossing itself, a distance of 250 feet. Viewing this film, it is easy to put oneself in the position of the unfortunate train driver on 8 November 1966, for whom, having put the brakes on, and with sparks flying off the train's wheels, the blocked crossing would still have been closing on him at the rate of at least 60 feet per second …

If, therefore, the Scammell rig did not clear the tracks until the final moment, as Phil Jones affirmed, then the train driver would have had the appalling sight of his way being obstructed as he ran onto the crossing. Those last three or four seconds, with an enormous crane jib clearly visible directly in front of him, must have been truly terrifying. No wonder he pulled up in Leominster Station and refused to go on.

Just how serious a collision would it have been if the train at Leominster had impacted, unslowed, with the laden Scammell rig? This is not just idle ghoulish speculation, for whoever awarded my father the equivalent of £80,000 in today's money certainly addressed this precise point. Two things are clearly different about the Leominster situation in comparison to Hixon: firstly, the locomotive at Leominster was far heavier, being a diesel, than the electrically powered Hixon locomotive; further, it would have been carrying a large amount of heavy fuel oil. Secondly, if the train's speed had been close to the prescribed 90 mph, then the point of impact would have been squarely on the middle part of the rig, where the body of the fifteen-ton mobile crane was located, giving a combined weight of over twenty-five tons, with that of the Scammell low-loader.

Putting these factors together leads to the sobering conclusion that the Leominster collision might have been much worse in its consequences than Hixon. Unforgiving physical laws take over in a situation such as this; in the opinion of one experienced fire and rescue officer, the engine of a diesel locomotive, impacting in these circumstances would have *exploded* and its heavy fuel oil ignited, engulfing the surrounding area in liquid flame. In fact, there is no need to rely on expert opinion on this matter because in 1984, British Railways deliberately ran a 112-ton, Class 47 diesel locomotive, at speed, into a substantial object, in this case a large steel flask weighing over thirty tons. The locomotive is doing over 90 mph and is pulling three carriages; sure enough, the locomotive explodes, sending out burning fuel oil for quite a distance around the point of impact.

Two other important differences with Hixon would have added to the mayhem at Leominster, because although there were only eight carriages behind the locomotive as compared to the twelve at Hixon, these would have been of an older, less robust pattern, rather than the new design of entirely steel construction, which were credited with saving many lives at Hixon. Added to which, this was a weekday (Tuesday) commuter train and it would likely have been filled with passengers. Also, unlike at Hixon, it was on the Down line and therefore the more crowded second-class carriages would have been at the front of the train. Finally, the cab of the Scammell was pulled up next to a house, which would surely have been seriously damaged, if not completely demolished by the encroaching wreckage of the train and lorry smashing into it. Even if the collision had resulted in only a moderately sized fireball, then it is unlikely that any of the railway personnel less than twenty yards away would have escaped unscathed; certainly crossing attendant Blower, on the signal-box steps, a mere twenty feet away from the stranded trailer, most likely wouldn't have survived,

Leominster, South End, signal-box as it was circa 1966, (and as it still is, pretty much, in 2017).

A Goods train running onto Leominster, Kington junction, level-crossing in the Autumn of 1966. In the background, a small phone cabinet is visible on the light-mast to the right of the photograph. It is under a sign-board, which has the single message: 'IN EMERGENCY PHONE SIGNALMAN'.

Phil Jones (left) and Jack Westwood sitting in Moreton-on-Lugg, signal-box, circa 1966.

A photograph of the wreckage of the locomotive and the first six coaches of the Express, taken from Hixon level-crossing looking South; probably late on the afternoon of Saturday, 6th January, 1968. The jib of a British Railways mobile crane and an emergency lighting tower can be seen behind the wreckage.

What appears to be part of the wrecked locomotive, again, the photograph probably taken on the afternoon of 6th January.

The train wreckage with the mobile crane and lighting tower visible in the foreground. This photograph taken looking North towards the crossing, probably on the afternoon of 6th January.

Part of the the mangled 'swan-neck' from the Wynns' transporter, next to the 120 ton transformer, the scrape marks on the bottom right of the transformer would seem to correspond to the wreckage of the 'swan-neck'. (This image was probably taken early on the morning of Sunday, 7th January, from the airfield side of the railway tracks, next to the Up-line, looking North).

More of the mangled 'swan-neck' in the foreground, with the British Railways recovery train alongside.

A photograph of the wreckage; judging from the presence of a fireman and the length of the shadows this must have been taken late on the Saturday afternoon.

In this photograph the transformer is about to be pulled over by the winch of the Wynns' forward 'Pacific' tractor, which is just out of shot to the right. The pulling blocks and cables are clearly visible. (H.P. Wynn is the figure in the Trilby hat close up to the transformer, and Gordon Wynn is at the extreme right of shot, with his back to the camera. The red crane in the background is the Wynns' ' iron fairy' brought in by H.P. Wynn. This image was definitely taken on the Sunday morning).

Taken a few seconds after the previous shot, the transformer has been pulled over onto its side.

A close up of the transformer. (The 'iron fairy's' jib is visible in the background).

Another close up from a different angle. (H.P. Wynn just walking out of shot on the left, Gordon Wynn on the extreme right).

This would seem to be back to Saturday afternoon, both the BBC vans and the British Railways' recovery workers standing around, would seem to indicate that the rescue of casualties and the retrieval of fatalities was still going on.

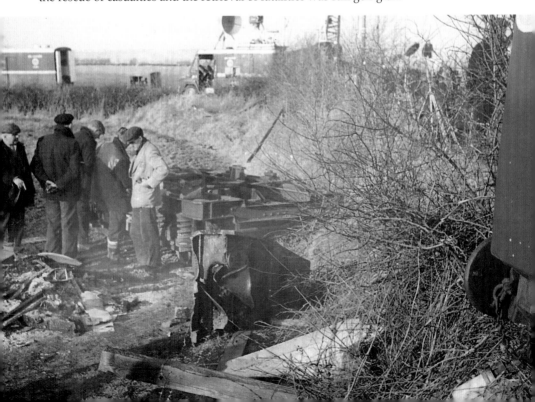

Again, the presence of police officers and the rescue lights would indicate this is Saturday afternoon.

The light quality indicates this is early Sunday morning, with the photograph being of the initial barrier warning sign on the approach down Station Road from the direction of the A 51. The railway's overhead catenary system is clearly visible in the background.

At the crossing, Sunday morning, before the transformer has been pulled over.

A photograph of the surviving barrier mechanism; note how hard to spot the telephone cabinet is on the rear of the mechanism housing. In the background, behind the lighting tower can be seen the transformer testing gear at the English Electric depot on the airfield.

This picture shows the 'Emergency Notice' sign-board, just visible against the white cottage behind it. It is clearly parallel to to the road carriageway and slightly bent over. This image was probably taken on the Sunday morning.

The Wynns' 'iron fairy' is present indicating it is early Sunday morning. Again the 'Emergency Notice sign-board can be seen, in its position of being parallel to the road carriageway. The BBC outside broadcast van has been moved up close to the crossing, which it certainly was not the previous day.

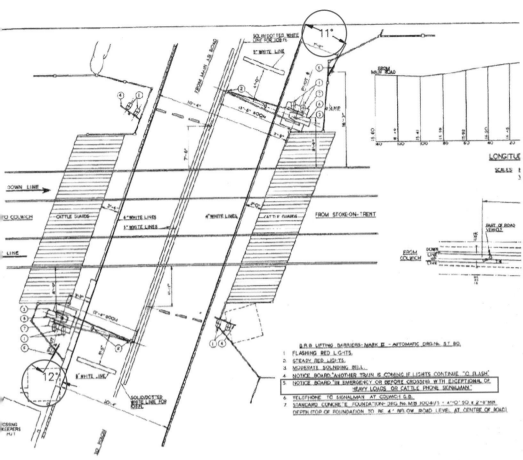

This is the installation diagram that the technicians installing Hixon crossing would have used when they were putting it in to place as an AHB crossing. It clearly shows both 'Emergency Notice' sign-boards at angles of 11 and 12 degrees to the road carriageway. The 'A 51 side' barrier is the one at the top of the diagram.

A photograph at Leominster level-crossing, taken looking North towards the Ludlow side on Tuesday 8th November, 2016, at 4.25 in the afternoon. As can be seen, the light is fading fast.

The same shot taken an hour later at 5.25 in the afternoon; that is 50 years to the exact time that the incident of Tuesday, 8th November, 1966 took place. The day light has virtually all disappeared.

The 'Hard facts on half-barriers' article, from *The Railway Gazette* of May 3rd 1968.

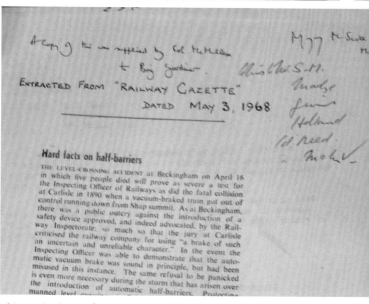

A copy of this was supplied by Col McMullen & Brig Gardiner.

EXTRACTED FROM "RAILWAY GAZETTE" DATED May 3, 1968

Hard facts on half-barriers

THE LEVEL-CROSSING ACCIDENT at Beckingham on April 16 in which five people died will prove as severe a test for the Inspecting Officer of Railways as did the fatal collision at Carlisle in 1890 when a vacuum-braked train got out of control running down from Shap summit. As at Beckingham, there was a public outcry against the introduction of a safety device approved, and indeed advocated, by the Railway Inspectorate; so much so that the jury at Carlisle criticised the railway company for using "a brake of such an uncertain and unreliable character." In the event the Inspecting Officer was able to demonstrate that the automatic vacuum brake was sound in principle, but had been misused in this instance. The same refusal to be panicked is even more necessary during the storm that has arisen over the introduction of automatic half-barriers. Protection manned level crossings...

The 'Chopping Block' article, from *The Daily Mail* of January 31st 1968.

DAILY MAIL, Wednesday, January 31, 1968

The chopping block

DOSSIER LISTS 18 INCIDENTS ON CROSSING

By REGINALD WHITE and DAVID JACK

A DOSSIER has been compiled of 18 accidents and incidents on a Continental-style l e v e l crossing known to train and lorry drivers as the 'chopping block.'

It will be put before railway, planning, and police officials next week. The crossing is on the busy A49 at Leominster, Herefordshire.

It was mentioned at the opening of the inquiry into the Hixon, Staffordshire, crash in which H ilford. Locals fear it could be the scene of another Hixon.

Next Wednesday, Mr. Thomas Gaylor, assistant chief constable of West Mercia police,

will meet British Rail divisional manager Mr C. A. Rose, the county surveyor, and Transport Ministry engineers to consider how the crossing might be made more safe.

The next day, Sir Clive Bossom, MP for Leominster, will ask Mrs Barbara Castle in the Commons to consider safety measures on the crossing.

'I want to get things moving,' he said yesterday. 'We can't wait until the Hixon report is published.'

These are three of the more serious of the incidents:—

Last Thursday: The brakes on Mr Kenneth

McLoughlin's 36ft articulator, laden with steel, jammed as he straddled the crossing. The barrier came down on the trailer as he heard a train approaching. Mr McLoughlin sprinted in the dark towards the oncoming goods train. The driver saw his torch signals.

May 1967: Tanker driver William Graham, crawling over the crossing behind a bus, was shocked when the barrier came down on his vehicle and warning lights started up.

He carried away the barrier poles as he inched off the crossing with an express roaring towards him. He just made it.

Mr Graham was prosecuted and acquitted

for driving through while the lights were flashing.

November 8, 1966: A driver employed by Wynns, Newport (the haulage firm involved in the Hixon crash), had trouble on the crossing while towing a heavy crane.

Three weeks ago deep snow put out of action the warning devices on the crossing. A police officer was posted to supervise traffic.

Mr Frank Webb, the magistrate who dealt with Mr Graham's case, said: 'People have told me this wretched crossing is not working properly.

'We have asked British Rail to look into the time factor linking lights, barriers, and arrival of trains. We have not heard from the Ministry or British Rail since our request for an inquiry into the incidents.'

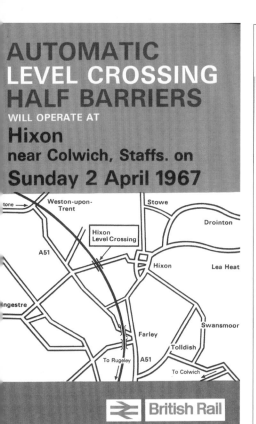

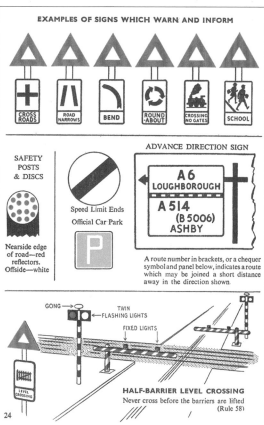

The front cover of the British Railways' public information leaflet from 1967, advising of the conversion of Hixon level-crossing to AHB working.

The diagram of an 'automatic crossing', from the 1959 (revised 1961) edition of *The Highway Code*, the one in use at the time of the Hixon disaster. As can be seen it is rudimentary in the extreme and nothing like what was in place by 1968.

An example of 'the reassuringly solid wooden gates', these are closed across the railway lines, leaving the road open for traffic to go on its way. (The crossing is at Blue Anchor station on the West Somerset Railway, in 2017.) Gates like these were standard across the country at controlled crossings, prior to conversion to AHB operation.
(Author's photograph)

TOTAL LENGTH 148 FT

The model of the actual transporter involved at Hixon, which was on display at the Inquiry hearings.

A photograph of Jack Westwood in his L.M.S Fireman's outfit, taken in 1945.

A painting reproduced by kind permission of the artist, Mike Jeffries, of a Wynns transporter negotiating a conventional manned level crossing at some time in the mid-1950s. Note the police motorcycle escort!

Wynns' Trailer '789'. This is the one that was taken 'empty' over Hixon crossing by Tommy Cromwell on Tuesday 5th December 1967, and taken over, loaded, with a 160 ton transformer on board, on Thursday 7th December 1967.
(This photograph dates from 1974, showing '789' negotiating a roundabout in Manchester. The transformer involved this time is slightly heavier at 177 tons.)

A Wynns' Scammell Highwayman low-loader, exactly similar to the one involved in the Leominster incident of 8th November 1966, but with a bulldozer on board rather than a mobile crane.

A Class 37 Diesel locomotive with a rake of 8 coaches on, drawn up in Hereford station. This is what the train involved in the Leominster incident of 8th November would have looked like. (Photograph by kind permission of Gordon Wood.)

Practical

Approachable

Reliable

Enthusiastic

Your Candidate

for Ward 2
Leominster

Bill
Sparey

A photograph of Bill Sparey, the Leominster farmer and NFU representative, who at the initial site-meeting in May 1965, successfully argued the case for a permanent telephone to be installed at Leominster, Kington junction, level-crossing. (Photograph by kind permission of the Sparey family.)

Some of the staff at Leominster station, late 1950s, probably on the occasion of a visit by Her Majesty the Queen and the Duke of Edinburgh. (The author's grandfather, Bert Pemberton, is on the extreme right.)
(Photograph by kind permission of Mrs J. R. Davies)

for even without any ensuing conflagration, the telescoping debris would have swept away both him and his box.

Thankfully, none of the above happened, at least not at Leominster. As now seems clear, this was entirely because of the actions of two ordinary working men, quickly sizing up a tricky situation and acting spontaneously and on their own initiative. Or did they? Certainly the lorry driver, James Horton, was expected by his employers, Wynns, to cope with unpredictable situations in precisely the way that he did at Leominster. Wynns stated as much to the Hixon Inquiry; as far as their own working practices were concerned they did not issue detailed instructions as to safety considerations, preferring instead to rely on the good sense of their intelligent and competent workforce. Strangely, with the Railway the exact opposite was the case: experience had shown that in emergency situations, such as a blocked permanent way, speed of response was of the essence and that therefore cutting out thinking time, if it could be done, was desirable. The relevant British Railways' safety instruction stated quite clearly that if a line is blocked, then the priority must be to get a message through to the covering signal-box, in the first instance, in order to prevent an accident if at all possible; but more importantly to ameliorate the situation by allowing signals to be put to 'danger', to isolate the point of blockage. So that, for example, a bad state of affairs is not made worse by a second train running onto wreckage. Secondly, once a message has been got through to the covering signal-box, or beforehand, if there are sufficient railway staff available, then they are to move rapidly along the lines either side of the blockage, towards any possible oncoming trains waving their arms above their heads, or red flags if they have them, in order to alert the train crew of danger ahead. Clearly, my father knew what had to be done and did it, sprinting across to the telephone on the warning light mast he had only recently helped install, and calling up the covering, signal-box.

Also, clearly, the senior railwayman present, S&T Inspector Hallett, did not think anything could be done, apparently not realizing until my father told him of his actions, that a call had been successfully made to put the signal to 'danger'. This explains why in his evidence to the Hixon Inquiry, James Horton was so scathing of Hallett's statement to him that the new AHB crossing was safe. When Horton spoke to him immediately after the incident, Hallett must have believed that the train had slowed *only* because the train driver saw the Scammell's trailer physically blocking the crossing, and that therefore although it had been a near squeak, the crossing had in fact operated as it was designed to do.

Whilst in retrospect, this attitude seems remarkably cavalier with railway safety, Hallett, as one of the railway's junior technical officers supervising the installation of AHB equipment, would have been assured by the Railway Inspectorate and his own immediate superiors that it was safe. Moreover, that the public would soon get used to them, and that the rank-and-file railwaymen were only interested in protecting outdated working practices. This set of attitudes was very powerful, 'strong magic' as it were, certainly powerful enough to make Hallett, in his turn, assure the lorry driver of the AHB crossing's safety, despite what both men had just witnessed, an assurance that was held up for much ridicule during the Hixon Inquiry's examination of what had occurred at Leominster. We must ourselves assume that Hallett knew nothing of my father's phone call, until he was informed of it a few moments after the lorry driver and his mate, drove off 'in high dudgeon' as Phil Jones described it. Indeed, until the unexpected and unwelcome appearance of the Scammell rig on the crossing, Hallett would have been quietly waiting for the express on the Down line to enable him to check that the crossing mechanism was functioning as it should have been; and therefore foremost in his mind would have been the paralyzing knowledge that once the barriers fell, the train would be on top of them in less than twenty seconds. Therefore, it is not at all surprising, that it is at this early point in the narrative that the suggestion that the train driver may have seen the obstruction on the crossing himself and applied the brake, is inserted. Largely because apparently, it did not enter Hallett's head that a phone call had been made. Remember that he thought my father had run off, to get out of harm's way. What is unforgivable, with no need for any benefit of hindsight, is that when young Inspector Hallett reported the Leominster events back to more senior British Railways' management, no investigation was mounted at the time, in November of 1966, neither was the information passed on as a matter of urgency to the Railway Inspectorate.

Another of my father's contemporaries on the railway, Mr Douglas Jukes, a former local magistrate and a retired signalman of many years' experience, some of it actually working in the Leominster South End box, confirmed to me that there would have been no shortage of written evidence as to what had occurred at Leominster crossing. He outlined the standard operating procedures as follows: first, any unscheduled halt within the Leominster Station track section, such as that by the express train, would have been written down in the box's Train Register; furthermore, the provision of a relief train driver would have generated another, separate, evidential paper trail at the Hereford Depot, starting with an entry in the local Movement Supervisor's log-book. Doug Jukes was very clear about the importance the Railway placed upon keeping full and proper records, with the Train Register ('The Bible') being regularly, but not predictably, examined and countersigned by an S&T inspector, in red ink. The added subtlety of making the Train Register inspection regime unpredictable, emphasizes the perceived need to keep the workforce 'on their toes', as it were. Every effort was made to provide operating systems that were as fool- (or knave-!) proof as was humanly attainable. Of course, all of this emphasis on the procedure of writing down events contemporaneously, had sagely been put into place over the years (largely at the instigation of the Railway

Inspectorate) in order to provide a reliable record of each and every movement on the rail network, thereby making investigation of any untoward incidents on the Railway as straightforward and therefore as expeditious as possible. It comes as no surprise to learn that the consequence for any signalman being found not to have made an entry into the Train Register, or to have made an incorrect entry, was a single warning and then, if something similar happened again, dismissal. This strict level of enforcement was of course necessary, if the Railways were to operate to the high standards expected of them by both the Railway Inspectorate and the public. However, the whole system quickly fell apart if information was not heeded and passed on when it needed to be. The question then becomes one of asking: why would any responsible British Railways' manager not pass on to the Railway Inspectorate details of teething problems with new, untested technology such as AHB equipped crossings? As we have seen in the previous chapter in the section dealing with Mr Lattimer's 'famous letter', the answer to that question lay in the nature and quality of the relationship between British Railways' management and the Inspectorate. Lattimer's decision was to not, personally, report the incident at Leominster and judging from surviving documentation of similar contacts he had with the Inspectorate over Leominster AHB crossing at around the same time, his reasons for not doing so seem entirely pusillanimous. In short, Lattimer was reluctant to upset the Inspectorate by raising concerns over their 'pet project', particularly as, when all was said and done, there had been no accident at Leominster. So, he chose not to officially inform the Inspectorate about the Leominster incident; instead he passed the matter over to his Divisional Management in Cardiff, to decide if they considered it necessary to take the matter any further.

Therefore, it was not until 23 February 1967, that a Mr Brennan, the then Movements Manager for the Welsh Marches line, made it his business to attend the commissioning site meeting for the Leominster AHB crossing and told Colonel Reed, face to face, what had occurred on 8 November, 1966. This was, of course well over three months after the event. The key fact to remember here is that the Inspectorate were never told officially of the Leominster incident. The necessary information was never written down and sent through the proper channels, meaning that Reed was the one, who now had to choose how he was going to handle the matter. In a way, Lattimer's stratagem worked brilliantly, at least in terms of the 'turf war' over telephones with the Railway Inspectorate: he had successfully passed the buck right back to where, in his opinion, it probably best belonged.

Chapter 5

The Chopping Block

*Events at Leominster, Kington junction, level-crossing,
subsequent to the incident of Tuesday, 8 November 1966*

A further document in the Ministry's 'Leominster' file is a letter to the Hixon Inquiry from a driver on the Cardiff to Crewe line, Mr R. J. Stuart. The letter is dated 28 February 1968, and having established his credentials as a senior express train driver, Stuart pulls no punches:

> I wish to call your attention to one of the Continental crossings between Hereford and Salop, Kington Crossing. I believe this is the crossing that has already been referred to at your inquiry. There is going to be a disaster here. Heavy bulk liquid tankers are using this crossing frequently and we are virtually clipping their tail lights as we go by. On two occasions my second man Peter Jones timed this crossing. From the time of sighting the arm dropping until I ran on to the crossing it was 12 seconds. On both occasions my speed was only 75 M.P.H. when it should have been 90. Anyone stalling on the crossing would not have time for a prayer much less time to push the vehicle off as suggested by that fool of a manager on Telly, and who could push a 50 ton tanker off?

This is self-evidently a stunningly powerful testimony, both the clear-sighted certainty of 'There is going to be a disaster here', and the information that his train was travelling well below its specified operating speed of 90 mph (this detail in particular, is later used to some effect by the chairman in the cross-examination of Colonel Reed of the Railway Inspectorate, who had claimed in one of his witness statements that the specified speed was 80 mph).

It is important to remember that the inquiry had commenced sitting in London on Monday, 26 February 1968, although Brian Gibbens, the chairman, had set out the terms of reference of the Inquiry a month earlier on Monday, 29 January, in Stafford. (This was designed to give enough time for each party summoned to the Inquiry, to submit the necessary documents, witness statements and list of proposed witnesses to the inquiry.) It seems clear that Mr Stuart was provoked into writing to the inquiry by what he had seen reported concerning the first two days of the resumed hearings, and particularly by information on Leominster crossing. His letter was taken extremely seriously and he was invited along to the Inquiry to give testimony in person.

There had been earlier disquieting information relating to Leominster in the national press, in particular an article in the *Daily Mail* of Wednesday, 31 January 1968 (*see* plate 25). Under a banner headline of 'The Chopping Block', the article claimed that there had been, 'eighteen accidents and incidents on a Continental-style level-crossing known to train and lorry-drivers as the 'chopping block''. What are referred to as 'three of the more serious of the incidents' are detailed: firstly, that which had occurred on 25 January 1968, when an articulated lorry carrying heavy steel plate, jammed across the crossing. Secondly, in May 1967, when a 50-ton tanker containing acid narrowly escaped being hit by an express train and finally the 'Wynns' incident' of 8 November 1966.

What is apparent from this is that the *Mail* was highlighting those incidents which clearly bore a resemblance to the Hixon accident, that is, the presence of a potentially train-wrecking obstruction on the crossing. It further mentions that Sir Clive Bossom, MP for Leominster, was to ask questions in Parliament seeking to persuade Minister of Transport Barbara Castle to take action regarding Leominster crossing straight away, 'I want to get things moving … We can't wait until the Hixon report is published.' The article goes on to refer to a dossier, detailing the eighteen accidents and incidents, being prepared for discussion at a meeting, which was to be held at Leominster Magistrates' Court the following week. The meeting had been called at the instigation of Assistant Chief Constable Gaylor of West Mercia Police. Attendees were representatives of British Railways, the Ministry of Transport's Divisional Road Engineering department, Herefordshire County Council, and the police. A full set of minutes exists of this meeting, which went forward to the Hixon Inquiry and was labelled as Document M 23, 'M' in this case stands for Ministry of Transport, so whereas the *Daily Mail* report may or may not have come to the attention of the Inquiry, the substance of what had been happening at Leominster crossing most certainly did. Probably the most important fact to take away from this meeting is that it was called by the police, who, judging from the minutes, were getting heartily fed up with being called out to incidents at this particular crossing, ever since it had been converted to automatic working in the autumn of 1966.

Assistant Chief Constable Gaylor detailed the numerous barrier failures and near collisions that the police were aware of; a Mr Rose, Assistant Divisional Manager for British Railways, replied that all the barrier failures had been 'to safety', that is, the barriers had stayed down across the carriageways. He went on to 'straight bat' the situation at the crossing, saying that the new AHB equipment 'was of a design approved and inspected by an Inspecting Officer of Railways' and that the crossing 'installation was covered by an order of the Ministry of Transport'.

This meeting is peculiar, in that it appears to have had no official status or consequence, both as far as the railway and Ministry of Transport were concerned. It was held 'in camera' and no details were released to the 'large number of reporters and press photographers' who had descended upon Leominster to cover it. Its primary purpose seems to have been to provide a résumé of events at Leominster crossing, in an appropriate and acceptable form to put before the Hixon Inquiry; that is, not just disparate newspaper reports, which could be dismissed as hearsay or ill-informed tittle-tattle. As far as Leominster crossing was concerned, in a way the meeting was a Convocation of Monkeys, because the Organ Grinders, that is the Railway Inspectorate, were not present. However, its effect was profound, in that the minutes were sent to the Hixon Inquiry, presumably by the senior Ministry of Transport official present at the meeting, Mr F. S. Alexander of the Divisional Road Engineering Department of the Ministry of Transport, which would explain their labelling as 'M 23'.

Several interesting pieces of information are contained within these minutes: first it is revealed that the two signals on the Down line protecting Leominster station track section had been, by early 1968 – in Colonel Reed's memorable phrase, 'done away with' – these were the ones that were deployed on 8 November 1966 to slow the oncoming passenger express. The nearest signal on the Down line was now at Wooferton some two miles 1,098 yards north of Leominster crossing. On the Up line there was, 'the control signal at Ford Bridge two miles 1,047 yard away from the crossing'. Thus we can see Colonel Reed's scheme for increasing the capacity of the line, referred to in chapter 1, had been implemented; the two multiple-aspect control signals were nearly five and a quarter miles apart, thereby facilitating express passenger trains to operate at the prescribed speed of 90 mph for longer. Of course, this new signalling disposition meant that my father's crucial phone call on 8 November 1966 would not have been possible.

Also fascinating, because of what it reveals about the state of knowledge and, more importantly thinking, at quite a senior level in British Railways' management concerning the safe operation of AHB crossings, is what Welsh Division Assistant Manager, Cliff Rose, had to say concerning the automatic half-barrier systems. Mr Rose said he considered – along with the Railway Inspectorate – 'that display of the flashing red lights to road drivers should be quite enough to provide safe operation of the level crossings. The half-barriers were provided for nothing more than psychological reasons.' Two things spring immediately to mind here; firstly, Rose is using the Inspectorate to support and justify what would have seemed (rightly!) at the time, an extraordinary departure from safe practice at level-crossings. Furthermore, for good measure, he slings in a little bit of jargon by describing the half-barriers as just being there for 'psychological reasons'. Rose plays no further part in events relating to Hixon, so no more time should be spent on his eccentric and at the time, untested views.

(Except to say that eighteen years later, in July 1986, an accident at a crossing protected by flashing lights alone, at Lockington in Yorkshire, cost eight lives: a passenger from the road vehicle and seven passengers on the train involved. The inquiry into that accident concluded that the driver of a Ford Escort van failed to see the flashing lights and drove into the path of an oncoming four-carriage diesel multiple unit, travelling at around 50 mph, causing the train to derail and partially fall down an embankment, hence the fatalities on the train. Flashing lights can have no protective effect, psychological or otherwise, if they are not seen. It is more than a little concerning that given the Hixon Inquiry's clear, unambiguous recommendations about the necessity for a full suite of warning devices – signs, lights, barriers – appropriately placed at public road crossings, that British Railways and the Railway Inspectorate had still pursued the dream of protecting busy road crossings, used by relatively fast trains, with flashing lights alone. The go-ahead for these Automatic Open Crossings (AOCRs) had been authorized by a joint working party of the Inspectorate and British Railways in 1978, chaired by Lieutenant-Colonel A. G. Townsend-Rose; by the time of the Lockington incident there were forty-four AOCRs. Not surprisingly, an independent inquiry was convened to prevent what was seen to be another potential instance of the Inspectorate investigating their own actions. This inquiry was headed up by Professor P. F. Stott, who reported within just under a year. It was not good news for AOCRs: they were effectively eliminated, and most of the forty-four installed were converted to AHB protection.)

The somewhat unorthodox 'Chopping Block' meeting at Leominster took place on 7 February 1968 and as well as convening in the magistrates' court those present went and inspected the level-crossing, as is attested to by a photograph which appeared in *The Times* the following day. As mentioned, the minutes were duly passed on to the Hixon Inquiry, though it is impossible to judge precisely when copies would have been made available to all parties represented at the inquiry. But it is possible to deduce that 'M 23', together with other pieces of written evidence, such as Leslie Lloyd's letter, would have been read by all interested parties during the first few days of the Hixon Inquiry's resumed hearings. These began in London on Monday, 26 February and by Thursday, 7 March, counsel for the Ministry of Transport had been obliged to execute what can best be described as a 'hand-brake turn' regarding the official account of incidents that had taken place at Leominster level-crossing since its conversion to AHB working in the autumn of 1966.

It is a pity that that 'M 23' did not refer in detail to one incident that had occurred on Sunday, 4 December 1966, the so-called 'Colonel Gower' incident, when Lieutenant-Colonel Gower, the Commandant of the Army Apprentices

College at Chepstow, together with his wife, had only narrowly avoided a grisly death through being alerted by temporary crossing attendant Austen Blower's frantic shouts and flailing arms from the steps of his 'signal-box'. The couple had already driven on to the apparently open crossing (the barriers were raised) and the car was across the Up line; fortunately Gower was able to stop in the nick of time, as a lone diesel locomotive, a so-called 'light engine', whizzed past the bonnet of their car, on the Down line. Added to which, a lorry driver approaching the open crossing from the other direction had seen the Gowers' car stopped on the crossing and had made an emergency stop, otherwise he would have driven into the path of the oncoming 'light engine'. Furthermore, another lorry in front of this one had managed to get across with just seconds to spare. (The locomotive was travelling at 80 mph, apparently in order to 'strike in' realistically, to test the AHB mechanism.) Thus the Gowers had observed, at extremely close quarters, all three of these high-speed opportunities for collision and violent death, on a Sunday morning in rural England. Not surprisingly, they decided to take things further and instructed a firm of solicitors to contact the Railway with a description of the near-fatal mayhem, a request for an explanation and a complaint relating to the, quite understandable, nervous shock Mrs Gower had sustained. As with the letter from Wynns of a couple of weeks earlier, the Gowers' correspondence was dealt with by the Assistant General Manager of Western Region, Mr H. M. Lattimer, who, as with the earlier Wynns' enquiry, decided not to inform the Railway Inspectorate of this very serious incident. However, this time, fortuitously, the news got through to them by a different route.

A version of the 'Gower' episode, without any names being mentioned, had got into the local and regional press around the time it happened, via two brief reports in the *Hereford Times* of Thursday, 8 December and crucially, the *Birmingham Post*, of Monday, 12 December 1966. Moreover, given what Chairman Gibbens said later in his opening remarks on the first day of the Hixon Inquiry, about demanding any necessary information from all parts of the Government apparatus that he needed to, it is a great pity that the inquiry was not alerted to pursue this particular incident, and its truly astonishing and illuminating evidence trail. Primarily, because even a cursory investigation would have exposed the corrosive and dangerous relationship between the Railway Inspectorate and the senior management of British Railways, Western Region. All of this information would have been available at the time in the files of the Ministry of Transport and British Railways, and could have been brought to light, by asking questions of the right people, if Gibbens had known where to look and who to ask.

Now, whilst the 'triple jeopardy' details of the 'Gower' incident are hair-raising enough, its real interest in terms of the Hixon Inquiry lies in the fact that, as with the 'Wynns' incident of 8 November, Mr Lattimer, the Assistant General

Manager of Western Region, did not report it to the Railway Inspectorate, as he clearly should have done. They did however get to find out about it, because the report from the *Birmingham Post* turns up as a cutting (dated 15 December) on a Ministry of Transport internal memo sheet, surrounded by surprised and irate hand-written comments from colonels McMullen and Reed and Under-Secretary Scott-Malden.

The main reason for their anger does not seem to concern the incident itself, but rather the fact that they, the three most senior people involved in AHB crossing installation, had only found out about it from a press report, two weeks after it had happened. It was decided that Colonel Reed would get on the case and demand a full report on the 'Gower' incident from Western Region, whilst Mr Scott-Malden revealed that he had already been on the phone to have some 'strong words' with Mr Lattimer. Quite what effect, if any, these 'strong words' had on Lattimer is hard to say. He certainly does not appear to have been brought into line by them, in that having been caught out in not informing the Railway Inspectorate about one serious incident at Leominster, he did not then reveal to them the even more serious incident that had occurred a few weeks earlier, on 8 November. There is written evidence that the one thing that really got the Inspectorate annoyed, was Lattimer using a reference about them to bolster his response to a concerned member of the public. (As he had done in a letter written to Colonel Gower's solicitors, in which he stated that the Gowers' complaint was 'sub judice', because the Railway Inspectorate *might* be called upon to hold an 'Official Enquiry' (sic). Here is Lattimer trying to wriggle off that particular hook, in a letter of 12 January 1967 to the Chief Inspector, Colonel McMullen: '[we] felt that the public and safety interest was best served at that stage by an intimation that it was in the hands of the highest possible authority appointed to look after it – in other words yourselves.' This grovelling tosh was written in response to a phone call from McMullen, who had been on the phone to Lattimer to tell him to desist from taking the Inspectorate's name in vain, presumably with an 'or else' if he didn't stop. Therefore, it does not seem unreasonable to conclude that Lattimer, conscious of his career prospects being at risk, chose not to reveal the 'Wynns' incident, because in his letter of 29 November to Wynns (the 'famous' letter, as Chairman Gibbens later referred to it) Lattimer had stressed that the AHB crossing was of a design approved by the Inspectorate, and that the Inspectorate would agree with him that Wynns were to blame for obstructing the crossing. Remember, that Lattimer had not intended to inform the Railway Inspectorate about *either* the 8 November *or* the 4 December incidents at Leominster. He was caught out regarding the latter, and must have feared that he would have got further into hot water if they had found out about him having already referred to them in his letter to Wynns. So apparently, for this most pusillanimous of reasons, safeguarding his own career, Lattimer never informed the Railway Inspectorate of the 'Wynns' incident, preferring instead to use references to them to try to impress and overawe complainants. A further indication of Lattimer's tendency to cobble together extremely dubious arguments in response to complainants, was his suggestion to Colonel and Mrs Gower that they should not be concerning themselves about problems with the level-crossing at Leominster ... because they lived over fifty miles away in Staffordshire!

What is quite damning as far as Colonel Reed – and by extension Colonel McMullen and Under-Secretary Scott-Malden – is concerned, is that in his witness statement of 8 March 1968, Reed says that British Railways Western Region informed the Inspectorate of the 'Gower' incident; no they did not. That information only came to light because the Inspectorate spotted the story in the *Birmingham Post* and had then to make inquiries themselves of Lattimer; if they had not done so they would have been none the wiser.

Chapter 6

The Hixon Inquiry gets under way and the Railway Inspectorate has a nasty shock

Of course other things had been happening as regards the subject of the inquiry; first off there was obviously intense public and media interest in the circumstances of the Hixon collision itself. Mr John Wynn, then a young man working for his family's firm, had set out from South Wales by car as soon as Wynns had received the dreadful news on Saturday, 6 January. It had been John who took the phone call from Bryn Groves, the driver of the lead tractor, and he recalled:

> The call from Bryn was quite short and matter-of-fact, 'There's been an awful smash, we've been hit by a train, all of the crew are O.K.' Of course, he must have been in shock. I found out where they were, spoke briefly to Uncle Percy [H. P. Wynn, a senior director] and then I set off in the firm's Rover. All the way up I had the radio on and there were numerous news updates, on what was already being described as a major disaster.

He got to the scene at about 2.30 in the afternoon and then faced a walk of around half a mile to the crossing itself, because the roadside was choked with the parked cars of people who had, presumably, come to see what they could of the wrecked train and the rescue operation. Noel Wynn and H. P. Wynn, the most experienced of the company's directors, arrived at Hixon later that afternoon at around 4.15 and immediately took stock of the scene of devastation, in particular measuring out exactly where the locomotive's point of impact had been on the trailer. H. P. Wynn offered road-borne heavy-lifting equipment to the railway authorities, to help deal with the wreckage caused by the collision, in particular moving the 120-ton transformer which had been thrown some twenty feet by the force of the collision. Unsurprisingly, the offer was gratefully accepted by the Railway. Having arranged for the arrival and bringing into use of a large crane from their Manchester depot for the following day, the three Wynn family members then drove four of the five-man crew of the wrecked transporter back to Newport, arriving late in the evening and delivering the badly shaken-up men to their families. (The fifth man, Alan Illsley, the driver of the rear tractor, lived in Manchester). Then at 6 the next morning, John, Noel and H. P., together with another director, Gordon Wynn, set off once more for Hixon, arriving just after 9.30.

They then spent the Sunday helping further with the clearance operation. That same Sunday evening the Minister of Transport, Barbara Castle, announced that the inquiry into the accident at Hixon was to be the first independent formal investigation into a railway accident since the Tay Bridge disaster of 1879. Her statement went on to say that this action had been taken because 'others besides railway employees were closely involved in the circumstances of the accident' and moreover that it was 'desirable to have an independent review of the use of the [automatic] half-barriers in British conditions'. Clearly, it was decided very early on, at the highest level, that the accident at Hixon should not, and would not, be dealt with in isolation. Moreover, there were to be no further AHB crossings installed until the inquiry had issued its findings. (The date for the inquiry's preliminary hearing was set for the 29 January in Stafford. Thereafter, and allowing a month for evidence to be collated and witnesses identified and summoned, the inquiry was moved to central London for the rest of its proceedings, resuming at 6, Burlington Gardens on 27 February.)

The four members of the Wynn family, H. P., Noel, Gordon, and John, heard the news of the form the inquiry was to take that Sunday, whilst they were still at the crossing and realized the firm would need expert legal representation. Late that evening, over the telephone, they secured the services of the solicitors A. E. Wyeth and Co., who specialized in industrial accidents and their aftermaths.

Perhaps surprisingly, long before the inquiry proper got under way there had already been two perfectly legitimate investigations into the course of events at Hixon on that fateful January Saturday. Firstly, British Railway's Divisional Operating Superintendent, for Stoke-on-Trent, Mr Robert Mackmurdie, held an investigation, as soon as practicable, on Monday, 8 January; this was limited to the questioning of and receiving reports from railway personnel only. (Mackmurdie's report was *not* passed on to the Hixon Inquiry however Mackmurdie himself was called as a witness before the Inquiry. He had arrived on the scene of the accident shortly before 5 p.m. on 6 January and then remained there for over twenty hours.)

The essentials of his initial findings were given to the assembled press on the afternoon of 8 January: 'Nothing has indicated there should be any recommendations about the operating of automatic barriers at crossings' and furthermore, 'Automatic half-barriers are sited and equipped to the requirements of the Ministry of Transport.' Together with these very circumspect statements the newspapers were able to print the much more graphic details supplied by railwaymen and others on the spot at the time of the collision. In particular the signalman on duty in the covering Colwich signal-box, Mr Brian Register, was able to confirm that he had not received any telephone call from anyone at Hixon crossing on the day of the accident, as was required by the signboard on display at the crossing. Not only had he not received any call on 6 January, but he revealed that he had not received any phone calls from the crossing, concerning exceptional loads, during the six months of its operation as an unmanned automatic crossing. (Although, as was established by the inquiry, there had in fact been one such phone call, on 7 December 1967, from a policeman escorting another Wynns' transporter, enquiring about the clearance under the 25-kilovolt wiring.)

Register's evidence, which he repeated at the Hixon Inquiry, seemed to penetrate directly to the causation of the Hixon collision. Why had neither Wynns' five-man crew or the two escorting police officers made a call to the supervising signal-box? This was the question which was quickly asked in the many newspaper articles written around the time. Signalman Register went on record in *The Daily Sketch* of Monday, 8 January, saying that he could so easily have averted disaster, if only he had been called.

The other investigation into events at Hixon crossing on 6 January was conducted by H. P. Wynn, based on observations and measurements he had made at the crossing on the Saturday and Sunday and from questioning the five Wynns' employees involved. The preliminary results were given to the press in a statement issued by A. E. Wyeth and Co, Wynns' solicitors, on Wednesday, 10 January. Wynns emphasized 'that the transporter had not stopped on the crossing at any time' and that 'on the contrary having followed the Police car on to the crossing the tractor crews remained at their posts and did their utmost by accelerating to get the transporter clear immediately the danger became apparent. Furthermore, at no time did any part of the vehicle or its load come into contact with the overhead wires'. It was also pointed out that the transporter had been following a route prescribed by the Ministry of Transport, which also required Wynns to inform the police 'with whose directions they were bound to comply'. Finally, the matter of telephoning the signal-box was raised, but with a markedly different emphasis: 'Questions will now arise as to the adequacy of the type and position of the British Railways notice requiring the signalman to be telephoned in special circumstances, of the telephone itself, and of the safety margin and precautions relative to this new type of crossing which are already the subject of public comment.'

There, in this last paragraph, were neatly delineated the essential matters that were to be examined by the Hixon Inquiry itself. Also, these two 'rival' preliminary investigations fitted in perfectly with the classic adversarial English legal procedures, that Mr Justice Gibbens had to employ to get to the truth of what had happened at Hixon crossing on the first Saturday of 1968. The 'third party' closely involved in the Hixon events, the Staffordshire Police, could also have conducted their own investigation, but chose not to do so. Although their Chief Constable, Arthur Rees, who had himself arrived at the scene of the collision within half an hour of it happening, went on the record in the Birmingham-based *Sunday Mercury* of 7 January, that the police escort for the

Wynns' transporter had not seen the signboard advising of the necessity of a telephone call to the covering signal-box, because:

> There is a sign by the crossing giving instructions for the crossing procedure for heavy loads but it does not face the oncoming traffic. It is doubtful if the sign could be seen by anyone driving a car or vehicle past it. If the sign had been facing oncoming traffic our driver would have seen it. He did see the warning sign which does face oncoming traffic on the other side of the road. The red warning lights showing that a train is approaching were not flashing.

The Chief Constable made these comments on the evening of the collision; the following morning (Sunday) he was back at the scene, and together with a reporter and photographer from the *Birmingham Post* examined the signboard, the result of this examination appearing as a front-page article on Monday, 8 January. The headline says, 'Sign that drivers may miss' and the reporter, Noel Thompson, then recounts how, having been told of the existence and nature of the signboard, he was unable to locate it and that it was only when he had it pointed out to him by Mr Rees that he saw it:

> [It] reads, 'In Emergency or before crossing with heavy or exceptional loads or cattle, phone the signalman'. I failed completely to spot the notice regarding the telephone. It does not face oncoming traffic, but across the road. All a driver could see is the thin edge of the metal plate [which carries] the wording.

Thompson goes on to say that he had no success locating the telephone in the barrier housing until that too was pointed out to him. Clearly, the Chief Constable was keen to get this information concerning the signboard and telephone into the public domain, but was mindful of not saying anything himself: 'Mr Rees would not give his opinion of the positioning of the notice.' "That is up to you" ', was all he said. Immediately after this interview the photographer took a shot of the signboard as it was. Then the two journalists saw something which concerned them enough to send a formal report in to the Hixon Inquiry. Thompson stated: 'Only a few minutes after the photo was taken, I saw a man wrestling with the sign and pole in what seemed to be an attempt to test its security, or to dislodge it. I do not know who the man was. The sign did not budge and at that stage it was left facing as I had originally seen it: parallel to the road.' The photographer, Alan Hill, said that he too saw the person 'apparently trying to shift the sign' and confirmed that it did not move position. When the two men were next present at Hixon crossing on the following Wednesday, 10 January, they immediately noted that 'the signboard was now facing towards oncoming road-users, having been turned round 90 degrees'. Now, although the person wrestling with the signboard around noon on the Sunday remained unidentified, paragraph 150 of the Hixon report states that Robert Mackmurdie, British Railway's Divisional Superintendent was 'obviously worried by the position of the Emergency Notice immediately after the accident because on the evening of the 6th of January he tried by hand whether it could be turned; but it did not move', Furthermore, Mackmurdie said on oath in his evidence, that back in September 1967 he had observed the Emergency Notice 'at an angle of 20 to 30 degrees', that is more or less, facing onto oncoming traffic. Was Mackmurdie 'obviously worried' on the evening of 6 January, because he realized that if the signboard was in the position that he had now found it to be, *at the time of the collision*, then it was virtually useless as far as being seen by approaching motorists was concerned. Hence his attempt to see 'whether it could be turned'.

The first day of the inquiry took place on 29 January amid a great deal of media interest, and the approach of one party to the proceedings, namely Wynns, was clearly to use the media to spotlight any issues that they believed might not get the attention they deserved at the inquiry. As a response to what they considered to be selective 'pre-releasing' of evidence by British Railways, Wynns released all the correspondence they had had with British Railways concerning AHB crossings (including, of course, Lattimer's letter), which correspondence, as *The Times* reported, 'seemed to show that British Railways were unhelpful to a haulage concern worried about automatic crossings'. Although the proceedings only lasted twenty-six minutes in total, Wynns' counsel, Patrick Bennett, managed to establish that the firm believed they were being 'set up' or in legal language 'entrapped' by British Railways. (Putting into the public domain this early on, that a nationalized industry might not be behaving properly was a very astute strategy, regardless of whether it was true or not. Don't forget that only a year beforehand, another nationalized industry, the National Coal Board, had been rightly castigated by the Aberfan Tribunal for its irresponsible and negligent behaviour in its approach to that tribunal's proceedings. As it turned out, British Railways probably wasn't attempting to entrap Wynns; on the other hand the Ministry of Transport certainly were!

During the first seven days of the hearings Chairman Gibbens found himself presiding over a concerted attempt by the barristers representing the Ministry of Transport to question the veracity of the evidence produced by Wynns concerning both the Hixon and Leominster incidents, to the extent that Wynns' legal team reiterated that the company felt that they were being 'entrapped in this situation'.

On the morning of Day Seven of the hearings the evidence of James Horton, Wynns' lorry driver at Leominster, was subjected to intense scrutiny, in particular what he remembered about the presence, or otherwise, of telephones and signage relating to telephones at the Leominster crossing. A statement was produced, taken from Horton's assistant lorry driver, a Mr Leslie John, which said that there *had* been a signboard visible at the crossing, that Horton claimed not to have seen. It seemed clear that the Ministry of Transport were intent on pinning as much of any blame that there was to be pinned onto Wynns' personnel, and the firm's working practices, on the basis that they had both been common factors at the Hixon disaster, and the earlier near-catastrophe at Leominster. Then a remarkable thing happened: just after the lunch recess, Mr Read, counsel for the Ministry of Transport, made the following statement:

> Perhaps I could make this clear; the evidence will establish it hereafter, but whilst you have the Leominster incident in mind, it is right I should tell the court my instructions are that at the time of this incident there was no telephone at the crossing, and therefore no telephone notice. The order which permitted the installation was made in September 1966 and did not specify a telephone; it is one of the very last ones that went up without telephones; but the telephone and notice were installed before Colonel Reed made his inspection in February 1967. In fact this was the interim period between the installation and the final siting of notices, so that it is fair to the driver to say he did not see a notice or telephone because there was none there in any event.

The Chairman, Brian Gibbens, immediately asked two questions, first: 'Was there any man on the level-crossing barrier, apart from the signalman in the box?' To which came the somewhat ambiguous answer: 'Only the railwaymen working on the Leominster side of the crossing.' Gibbens tried again: 'There was no one attending to the crossing?' This time a straightforward: 'No, sir.' (I must confess to having a lump in the throat when I first read this part of the transcript, because I knew that there had indeed been someone 'attending to the crossing': my father.)

It is often said that it is good courtroom technique to only ask questions to which you already know the answers; Gibbens knew that the answers he had received, given on behalf of the Ministry of Transport, specifically the Railway Inspectorate, were in direct contradiction to the detailed witness statement of Leslie Lloyd, the Movements Manager for British Railways Western Region. Of course Lloyd's witness statement 'proof' would have been made available to all the parties represented at the inquiry, so presumably, the Railway Inspectorate must also have received their copy sometime during the morning of Day Seven of proceedings, hence their decision to make a statement, this time in direct contradiction of the case their legal team had been making for the previous six and a half days. The only plausible reason that they would have done this is that initially, on Day One of the Inquiry hearings, the Ministry's legal team had been instructed that because the Leominster crossing had been converted in

October 1966, after phones had been made compulsory at all AHBs, therefore there were both phones for the use of the public and notices at it. However, upon seeing a copy of Leslie Lloyd's witness statement on the morning of Day Seven, somebody, presumably Colonel Reed, must have then realized that the crossing was *authorized* in September 1966 and therefore assumed that British Railways had obeyed his instructions and only provided 'plug-in' sockets for railway use, as was stated in the crossing's authorization documents.

Hence, although it pretty much trashed the Ministry's initial case against Wynns, the only thing to be done was to state that there were no phones. The statement read out by Mr Read, the Ministry barrister, was a holding statement, containing the essentially correct information that there were no 'public phones' or notices, but as Chairman Gibbens's two perceptive questions pointed up, it was not entirely accurate. Gibbens clearly smelt a rat as far as the Ministry's pursuit of James Horton, Wynns' lorry driver at Leominster, was concerned, and allowed him to withdraw from the inquiry, with the words: 'Mr Horton, it is quite clear you did a very good job on that day, and as far as we can see you saved a very serious accident. Thank you very much.' (To my knowledge this is the only public recognition Horton ever received for his exceptional and selfless bravery.)

At this point, on Day Seven of the hearing, Gibbens also closed off any further investigation of what had actually occurred at Leominster on 8 November 1966, as he put it, 'No one has really challenged Mr Horton's evidence.' As it turns out, Mr Read's statement is doubly misleading because as well as stating that there were no telephones installed, it implies that there had been a conscious decision made in September 1966, to have no telephones at Leominster crossing, in a straightforward way, and in line with the enabling legislation in force at the time and agreed with by British Railways. Nothing could be further from the truth. Colonel Reed might have thought he had authorized an AHB crossing without telephones at Leominster; what he had not bargained on was that British Railways had installed a single phone, on one of the warning light masts, in line with a request from the National Farmers' Union representatives, at the initial site meeting back in May 1965. At Leominster crossing on 8 November 1966, Wynns and their lorry driver, Horton, were just innocents caught up in the shambolic, and soon to be tragically lethal, AHB crossing installation process.

Now, sixteen months later at the inquiry hearings, in open court session, the astonished, but attentive, counsel and representatives of Wynns had just observed the Ministry of Transport admitting a gross error as to the state of affairs at Leominster crossing. On which state of affairs, they had based suggestions of incompetence and recklessness against James Horton and by extension negligence and incompetence by Wynns as his employers. Significantly, it seemed to play to the assertion that Wynns had made that they were being 'entrapped' by less than scrupulous government agencies. Wynns would also have noticed that the chairman had smartly moved things on and accepted Horton's account of events at Leominster; he and his employers, Wynns, were certainly not the ones displaying incompetence or recklessness. That dubious accolade clearly lay elsewhere.

At the start of proceedings on the following morning, Wynns' leading barrister, Morris Finer, made a statement to the inquiry which whilst maintaining the view that Wynns had been 'entrapped' by the circumstances relating to the Leominster incident, then went on to say:

> However, there are some traps which greater fore-sight can avoid, and I would therefore like to make it clear at this stage, and to do so without reservation, that Wynns do fully recognize that on receipt from their driver Horton of his report of the incident at Leominster on the 8 November 1966 they ought to have realized, although in fact they did not do so, the serious implications for their operations in general … in particular, to have taken steps to have put all their employees on warning, and, despite the remarkable response … of British Railways to the approach that was made to them, to have done more to pursue the matter.

So, whilst not withdrawing from their assertion that the Railway authorities had been seeking to entrap them, Wynns acknowledged that they should have acted differently, and therefore also acknowledged a partial responsibility for the circumstances that brought about the Hixon disaster. In his evidence Noel Wynn, who had dealt with Lattimer's 'famous' letter stated "that in a sense it allayed my concerns", Wynns had apparently believed that the situation at AHB crossings was not as dangerous as Horton had told them it was. Now, they had seen their driver's account totally vindicated, and it was the realization of how much of a hazard their firm's employees had been in that prompted their statement. On the face of it, Wynns and their legal team clearly thought that the time had come to admit an honest but regrettable mistake. (They had, after all, the example in front of them of the Ministry admitting at the start of the inquiry that during the previous twelve years the 'steps which were taken' by the Ministry to ensure that the AHB crossings could be used safely by abnormal loads 'were not sufficient'. However, was this admission, by Wynns, of even partial culpability wise?)

What is truly remarkable is that Wynns' claim that a nationalized industry, together with part of the Ministry of Transport, had been seeking to entrap them, was allowed to stand un-investigated, therefore neither proven nor disproven. One obvious conclusion to draw from this, is that if the matter *had* been investigated, with full disclosure in open court of all the relevant documents and witnesses being examined under oath, then there was a very good chance that Wynns would have been able to prove their assertion, or that, at the very least, the chairman believed that they *might* be able to do so. He would also have been acutely conscious that the issue of what had occurred at Leominster, whilst crucial to an understanding of the botched process of automatic level-crossing installation, was probably peripheral to the causation of the Hixon collision itself. Also, Gibbens knew that the longer the delay to his Inquiry issuing its findings, the greater the risk of further accidents; far better to compromise with Wynns and press on with the main business. Which is what I believe he did.

In point of fact, of course, the chairman had documents in the inquiry's possession, which indicated not that the Railway Inspectorate and British Railways had been seeking to 'entrap' Wynns but that they had been at loggerheads over the Leominster crossing. In particular a letter from British Railways' chief solicitor, Mr Gilmour, dated 28 March,1968, makes reference to the Chief Inspecting Officer, Colonel McMullen, criticizing British Railways for allowing the Leominster crossing to operate in an unsafe condition. The letter alludes to what British Railways' response was to be when they gave their evidence, which was that Colonel Reed had inspected the crossing on 23 February 1967, and signed it off as safe to operate on 3 March 1967. Moreover, British Railways maintained that Reed was made fully aware of the events of 8 November 1966, during his inspection at Leominster. All of this information was included in Leslie Lloyd's letter which seems to have been *provoked* as to its content by Colonel McMullen's decision to try to blame British Railways for allowing the Leominster AHB crossing to operate with an unsafe road surface. A decision had clearly been taken by British Railways' most senior management that enough was enough: they were not prepared to allow the Inspectorate to offload responsibility onto the railway; it was indisputable that the crossing at Leominster had been inspected by Colonel Reed and had been approved. Furthermore, Lloyd's statement provided a full description of events at Leominster on 8 November 1966, and stated that Colonel Reed had been made aware of these events ten months before the Hixon collision and had taken no action, indicating a grave dereliction of duty on his part. As well as the chairman, of course, all of the other parties at the inquiry had a copy of Lloyd's statement.

Chairman Gibbens knew his primary duty well, because he was also aware that between them British Railways and the Railway Inspectorate had effectively put into place a gigantic 'Murphy's Law' experiment across the country: nearly 200 of the new automatic crossings were continuing to operate, each one, as far as anyone knew, potentially another Hixon, and worse still, nearly ten per cent of them without *any* telephones for the public to contact the railway in either an emergency or as a necessary precaution, although of course there were sockets for S&T Department 'plug-in' phones. One might be forgiven for assuming that the crossings without telephones were amongst the earliest ones installed, in the early 1960s. That is what is also implied in the Ministry of Transport counsel's statement, quoted in full above, 'it [the Leominster crossing] is one of the very last that went up without telephones'. So, the statement is doubly mendacious, because the reverse of this is closer to the truth: the crossings without telephones were *amongst those installed after 1963.*

The reality was that the May 1958, August 1959 and April 1962 provisional requirements of the Ministry of Transport authorizing the installation of AHB equipment, had specified telephones for the use of the public at all of the automatic crossings. It was legislation in 1963 that first gave the railway authorities the option of not putting in telephones, reinforced by more such legislation in 1966. In fact the 1966 legislation is reproduced in an appendix to the *Hixon Inquiry Report* itself. British Railways were supposed to make the case as to why each individual AHB crossing needed to have telephones for the use of the public; then the crossing would be approved by the Railway Inspectorate for conversion, with phones if a case had been successfully made, or without if not.

That was the theory of it anyway; the reality seems to have been that British Railways went along with the 1963 Conditions, up to a point, whilst trying to ensure that as many of the AHB crossings had a phone, of some sort, as possible. Whether an AHB crossing had telephones installed seems also to have been dependent upon which region of the rail network it was in; those regions where the management was less compliant to the wishes of the Inspectorate, were already doing their best to ensure the new crossings had telephones, and, what is more, were producing suitable signage to get the appropriate message across to the vehicle-driving public. This can clearly be seen in plate 2 which shows Leominster crossing just after conversion in October 1966, with the small phone cabinet mounted on the warning light mast and a simple, 'IN EMERGENCY – PHONE SIGNALMAN' signboard mounted just above it, with just those four words, correctly oriented to be nearly parallel to the carriageway, and therefore immediately readable to anyone who happened to be stranded on the crossing. Leominster was lucky of course, because it was on a trunk road, and therefore its signage was determined by Mr Alexander of the Roads Engineering Division of the Ministry, not by Colonel Reed of the Inspectorate.

The newly tightened Conditions issued by the Inspectorate / Ministry of Transport in July of 1966 seem to have been something of a final straw for British Railways' senior management at a national level, who decided from that point to instruct their regions to install AHB crossings with integral phones within each barrier housing. This explains why there was a duplication of provision at Hixon crossing (for example): a single phone on a post, next to the crossing keeper's hut on the airfield side of the crossing, plus two phones, one in each barrier housing on either side of the crossing. The single phone was retained from when the crossing had been fully gated and manned, because there was no signal-box at Hixon crossing itself; despite it being described as a signal-box in the *Hixon Inquiry Report*, it was just a small shelter for the crossing keeper.

It is instructive and somewhat sobering to read the July 1966 Conditions, in particular here is Condition 18 (Telephones) in full:

(a) If abnormal loads or cattle pass over the crossing frequently a telephone available to the public may be necessary. A notice displaying the words 'In Emergency or before crossing with exceptional or heavy loads or cattle, telephone signalman' will also be required. The notice boards to be reflectorised. The door of the cabinet containing the telephone to be marked in reflectorised material with either the word 'Telephone' or the appropriate symbol.

(b) If a telephone is not required, 'Plug-in' connections to be provided for an emergency telephone to be connected at site by railway staff when required for emergency working or maintenance.

(c) A suitable notice to tell road users how to contact the Railway in an emergency should be provided at all crossings where a special telephone is not required.

Of course, in the light of what happened at Hixon, and the catastrophe that would have happened at Leominster if there had been no telephone instantly available, the thinking behind not having telephones at AHB crossings is hard to fathom. One man in particular, Colonel Reed, was behind the move towards erecting automatic crossings without telephones; his opinion, succinctly put, was that they were unlikely to be of any use if a vehicle was stuck on an AHB crossing, and that, therefore, there was no point in having them. As has been pointed out above, what had actually occurred during the time that Reed was in charge of crossing installation, between November 1961 and early 1968, was that legislation had been put into place in 1963 (and 1966) that specified the option for crossings without publicly accessible telephones. There can be little doubt that Reed himself was the prime mover behind this legislation enabling AHB crossings without telephones, and that the eighteen or so such crossings which were installed, were authorized by him.

In his own evidence to the Hixon Inquiry and therefore under oath, Reed maintained that he had not been informed by British Railways of the events of 8 November 1966 at his 'signing off' inspection of Leominster crossing on 23 February 1967. It was a case of one man's word against another and despite an assurance from the barrister representing British Railways that they would produce an attested proof from Mr Brennan, the Movements Manager concerned, this does not seem to have been forthcoming. Although precisely the same information is contained in Leslie Lloyd's – the other British Railways Western Region Movements Manager – witness statement, which was available to the inquiry and certainly read by all concerned, it was never tested in open court by calling Lloyd as a witness. Lloyd was

Movements Manager at the time of the Hixon Inquiry in 1968, but at the time of the 'signing off ' inspection in February 1967 the Movements Manager was Brennan who was based in Cardiff. He would have had to come up to Leominster to attend the meeting and it would have been something out of the ordinary for a movements manager to attend such a meeting. Usually a less senior, more locally based officer from that section would have attended, such as the Movements Supervisor based in Hereford. One plausible explanation as to why Brennan attended is that he had something he wanted to make sure was said to Colonel Reed, presumably about what had occurred back in the November of 1966 when, as we now know, one of the train drivers for whom Brennan had overall responsibility had brought his train to an unscheduled halt in Leominster station and refused to continue. This, after only narrowly avoiding colliding with the Wynns' Scammell rig. From what we have already seen about the unequal relationship between British Railways' management and the Railway Inspectorate, then I suspect it took not a little personal resolve, if not actual courage to go and beard Reed on his home ground, as it were. If we assume, for the sake of argument, that Reed *was* told by Brennan, then what should he have done about it ?

He should have held a serious incident investigation of course, and initially that is what I thought he had done, presumably between the inspection at Leominster on Thursday, 23 February and the final signing off of the crossing on Friday, 3 March. However, Reed's response during his cross-examination at the Hixon Inquiry, just over one year later, to being asked whether he remembered being spoken to by Brennan was a puzzled, 'In what context?', followed by a trenchant denial that he had ever spoken to any of the railway officials about the events of 8 November 1966, prior to the Hixon collision. It makes complete sense knowing what we know happened ten months later, that Reed should have held an investigation; this is not hindsight. If Reed had been doing his job properly he ought not to have dismissed Brennan's concerns in the manner he apparently did, but he was not being objective about AHB crossings; in effect he was their chief advocate. So this verbal report from Brennan, detailing a hair-raising near-miss seems barely to have impinged on Reed's consciousness; in the last analysis there had been no collision. Moreover, Reed and his two senior colleagues at the Ministry of Transport, Colonel McMullen and Mr Scott-Malden *had*, of course, 'rooted out' information about a slightly more recent incident at Leominster, the 'Colonel Gower' incident of 4 December 1966, from Mr Lattimer, Brennan's boss on the Western Region. Possibly, Reed's thinking on the matter, if there was any, was along the lines of, 'Well, this incident Brennan talks about can't have been that serious, or Lattimer would have mentioned it, along with the Gower incident.' As we have seen already, Lattimer had his own career-related reasons for not mentioning the incident of 8 November 1966 to the Railway Inspectorate.

The fact was that the dual roles of the Inspectorate in supervising the installation programme for AHB crossings and also being responsible for monitoring any potential safety issues were inimical to each other. Chairman Gibbens of the Hixon Inquiry never really 'got' this, or at least he does not mention it in his report, as the obvious principal and overarching reason for the safety issues with AHB installations. Again hindsight is not being deployed here; there were those at the time who clearly saw what had been happening, and as we shall see in chapter 10 took appropriate action to make sure it could not happen again.

As far as the Railway Inspectorate and their input into safety at the AHB crossings were concerned, right up until the Hixon collision, they were focused, to the point of obsession, with the possibility of 'poor discipline' amongst road users causing problems at the new crossings. There are documents relating to prosecutions of drivers at Leominster Magistrates' Court during 1967 and from their comments it is clear that various members of the Railway Inspectorate, Reed prominent amongst them, wanted to make sure that any malefactors as they perceived them, were found guilty and suitably punished. This was seen by the Inspectorate as part of the necessary process of educating the public as to the reality of the changed situation at level-crossings; but they hadn't told the magistrates this, who evidently still thought they were deciding each case on its merits. The Inspectorate became very annoyed if the local Bench took the side of the motorist against the railway and 'let them off', as happened when crossing attendant Austen Blower said that a Mr Graham, the driver of a fifty-ton tanker carrying industrial acid, had started across after the barriers had begun to descend; Mr Graham said he hadn't, he had merely been *proceeding cautiously* following a slowly moving bus in front of him and because the nature of his considerable load obliged him *to go slowly over the crossing.* (An express train had missed the back of the tanker by a foot or so; it emerged that the tanker had taken around fifteen seconds to clear the crossing, and the train had only been eighteen seconds away when the bells began to jangle and the lights to flash.) All the way through this cautionary tale of the installation of AHB crossings we have these little nuggets of information that were in front of Reed and his colleagues, but which were ignored; because the Inspectorate, instead of looking impartially at the way in which the public were dealing with the automatic crossings, were instead acting as the chief zealots in favour of them, and had already predefined any problems that were arising as being caused by 'poor discipline' amongst the public. The acid tanker incident and the subsequent failed prosecution of Mr Graham for 'Driving without due care and attention' did provoke some unease in Mr Ibbotson, the General Manager of Western Region, who sent a letter to the Inspectorate dated 22 May 1967, in which he drew their attention to 'the implications with regard to the safe working of the Railway where two trains pass over a crossing within a short period cannot be overlooked'. He also stated that he was referring the matter on to British Railways' chief legal adviser.

This was a 'critical second train situation', which the Inspectorate had now been informed about; eleven months *before* a similar occurrence cost five lives at Beckingham in Lincolnshire. Also of course, even disregarding the 'second train' element, the slowly moving acid tanker was a clear precursor of the slowly moving indivisible load at Hixon … if the Inspectorate had been open to such information. (Needless to say, Ibbotson's letter of 22 May 1967 never came to the attention of the Hixon Inquiry.)

Before moving on, it is worth pursuing these prosecutions of motorists a little more, because they illuminate quite well the fuzzy thinking in the Inspectorate behind the introduction of automatic *unmanned* crossings: Austen Blower, and his equivalents up and down the country, were only in place as attendants for a limited amount of time. This was usually from when the crossings had been installed and were functioning, to when they had received their 'signing off' inspection, typically between three to four months; after all the main reason for automating them was 'to save attendance', as Colonel Reed forthrightly stated in his model speech for initial site meetings. On the face of it, having a railwayman present at a recently converted crossing must have seemed like a good way of easing the transition between the old manner of protecting the crossing and the new. In reality, however, all it tended to do was point up the powerlessness of the Railway under the new dispensation: virtually complete control of events at the old gated level-crossings had been exchanged for no real control at all. Once an oncoming train had activated the crossing's mechanism it was likely to be occupying the crossing in less than half a minute. Moreover, as has been discussed earlier, whether a road vehicle stayed put or proceeded onto the railway lines in front of it, was now entirely the driver's decision. This was the precise situation that the Railway Inspectorate wanted; indeed by 1967, they had been working assiduously for well over a decade to bring it about. However a perusal of their various letters and memos written in connection with the prosecutions of motorists at Leominster reveals high levels of irritation if not downright anger, that some vehicle drivers were not doing what they were supposed to do. Maybe a bit of objective analysis of *possible* reasons why the drivers were apparently misbehaving might have triggered a realization that 'poor discipline' was not the only cause for concern at the new crossings. Unfortunately this did not happen, apparently because of Reed and the rest of the Inspectorate's certainty that AHB crossings were at least as safe as the old fully gated variety. This certainty was underpinned by the statistical analysis that had been carried out, that contrasted the comparatively tiny total amount of road carriageway there was at level-crossings, with the 200,000 miles of carriageway of Britain's entire road network, and worked on the assumption that there was no more likelihood of vehicles stalling whilst on a level-crossing than anywhere else on the road network. Hence the view expressed in Lattimer's egregious letter, that the possibility of a vehicle accidentally coming to a halt on a crossing was 'too remote to be contemplated'. That was what he had been told by the 'Masters of the Universe' (well, masters of his universe anyway) who were responsible for installing the AHB-equipped crossings and that was good enough for him. Powerful magic indeed, which held nearly all of the British Railways' senior management and the Railway Inspectorate / Ministry of Transport in its thrall until the Hixon Inquiry established its falsity. Nearly all, but thankfully not *quite* all, as far as those at the top of British Railways were concerned.

The clincher as to when a British Railways investigation of the Leominster incident was held, which was certainly no later than the spring of 1967, comes not from any document in the National Archive but from a lock-up garage rent book that belonged to my father. The first payment in the book is for June 1967 and he needed the garage for the car he had just purchased, a three-year-old Vauxhall Viva HB, registration number: BUX757B. It was my family's very first car and was bought before my father had passed his driving test. I was with him when he went to pick it up on 21 June (which was my birthday) and I remember he paid cash for it: £450 peeled off from a wad he took out of his back pocket. The salesman drove the car round to the garage, but my father parked it inside. (He passed his driving test, first time, after only six lessons a few weeks later, which was quite impressive for a 43-year-old.) Now the thing is, where did that wad of cash come from? We had no wealthy relatives and my careful parents would never have borrowed such a sum as large as £450, the equivalent of over £7,000 today. My further recollection is that for two or three years around this time we took our summer holidays at Llandudno hotels rather than the seaside caravan sites we had previously favoured. My view is that my father was given some of the £5,000 he had been awarded, probably £1,000, at or around the time that he gave his evidence to an investigation held in the spring of 1967. The bare details he could recall in 1987 tend to back this up: he was called up to Reading (where the S&T Department had their training school) and was told by a former Royal Engineers officer that his actions, independent of, but together with, those of Horton the lorry driver, had prevented a very serious accident. The question arises: if it wasn't Colonel Reed, as I had originally assumed, who gave my father £5,000 in total and quizzed him about his war service record, then who was it?

After considering the few attendant facts I was sure of relating to the events at Leominster crossing, I came to the firm conclusion that it could only have been Mr John Tyler, Chief Signal and Telecommunications Engineer of British Railways. Firstly, Tyler was a former Royal Engineers officer, holding the rank of lieutenant-colonel, had he cared to use it (which, refreshingly, he did not). Secondly, Reading was his headquarters, and finally, only someone close to the top in British Railways would have been able to hand out the equivalent of £80,000 in today's money. There is also compelling circumstantial evidence to support this conclusion, in that it was Tyler who had insisted upon telephones for the use of the public at each AHB crossing from October 1966 onwards, thereby overruling

Colonel Reed's intention of having no telephones as the standard option in the Ministry of Transport's revised AHB installation Requirements of July 1966. As the man ultimately responsible, and therefore answerable, for all works carried out by the S&T Department, Tyler would have had a clear motive for holding his own internal investigation into the events at Leominster crossing. Moreover, in terms of correct railway operating procedure he would have wanted to make sure that there was no possibility of disciplinary action being necessary against any railway personnel. Having observed that Western Region management had not referred the matter to the Inspectorate, and being in possession of S&T Inspector Hallett's initial report, Tyler would then have held his investigation, probably in the early spring of 1967, although it may have been earlier. (Since starting this book I have regularly checked and discussed the emerging content with several former railwaymen. One of them had initially been rather sceptical of aspects of the story; in particular he was taken aback by the way in which the Railway Inspectorate appeared to have put aside their usual close attention to safety, as far as AHB crossings were concerned. When I told him that in my opinion the Leominster incident had been investigated by Tyler at Reading, his reaction was, 'At last! Somebody in railway management correctly following procedure. It makes sense that the S&T Department would have wanted to check that there were no disciplinary matters to be dealt with, and that all of their men had acted properly in the circumstances.') When Tyler came to give evidence to the Hixon Inquiry on 20 May 1968, he was speaking with the full authority of the British Railways Board when he said that the Board did not like partial protection on half-barrier level-crossings. He was being cross-examined by Mr Read, counsel for the Ministry of Transport, who asked whether it was the case that the Board would not be prepared to put up many new half-barrier crossings unless some help was given with the cost of full protection. Tyler replied: 'We hope for the assistance of the court. If full protection was recommended we would hope for some relief. If partial protection is decided by the court, we would have to accept it, but we do not like it. We think it is wrong in principle.'

There we have it clearly delineated, and the chasm between British Railways and the Railway Inspectorate / Railways Group at the Ministry of Transport is revealed. What was not revealed, of course, was that Tyler was probably basing his assertion that AHB crossings as they were presently constituted, were 'wrong in principle' upon an investigation of the Leominster incident he had carried out several months before the Hixon disaster. In retrospect there would seem to be a significant moral dilemma for Tyler here: should he have told the Hixon Inquiry that he had carried out such an investigation? The fact is that he did not tell the Inquiry, but the information that he had gleaned about the Leominster incident was used to inform the witness statement of Leslie Lloyd, the Movements Manager of Western Region. (The idea that there *had* been an investigation by British Railways must have leaked out at some point because it is suggested in court papers dating from 1974, when the various parties to the Hixon collision – Wynns, British Railways, Staffordshire Police and the Ministry of Transport – were still engaged in preparing potential litigation against each other, a kind of 'Mexican stand-off' around who was financially liable for the disaster. The matter never did come in front of a Judge and was eventually settled, out of court, in 1977. In one of their defence submissions, admitted as evidence (that is, put forward to the court) by Staffordshire Police, it says this, referring to British Railways:

> [they had] failed to consider properly or at all the implications of the incident at Leominster on November 8th, 1966 ... which said incident was witnessed by their employees at the scene and reported in writing; *alternatively, if (which is not admitted) the implications of the said incident were appreciated, failed to take due or any precautions ...* [my italics]

This is fascinating, because by using the phrase 'which is not admitted' Staffordshire Police are saying that they don't have any evidence to hand, but that they have reason to believe that such evidence would come to light, if the matter were to be revisited by a court.

As far as the author of this book is concerned, having looked at the matter of the Hixon disaster and inquiry, informed by the unique perspective that my father's story has given me, I would put forward the following: first, a state of hostility existed between the Railway Inspectorate and the senior management of the Signal and Telecommunications Department of British Railways; the reason for this unhappy state of affairs, in brief, was the manner in which AHB crossings had been introduced. In particular, during the 'spurt' in installations that took place from 1963 onwards, when as has been discussed already, the mandatory inclusion of phones at crossings for the use of the public, had been waived in favour of no phones, unless a need could be demonstrated. This was anathema to the S&T Department and when the restriction on phones was strengthened in the Ministry's July 1966 Requirements, that was when Tyler as chief of S&T operations insisted on phones at each crossing.

Secondly, when after the Hixon disaster it became plain to the senior management nationally of British Railways, that the Chief Inspecting Officer, Colonel McMullen, intended to blame British Railways for aspects of AHB crossing installation that were not their responsibility, they decided to point out to the Inquiry an instance where the Inspectorate, particularly Colonel Reed, had been given information upon which they should have acted, but did not do so. In other words, the pre-existing hostility between the Inspectorate and the S&T Department spilled over into the Inquiry.

Thirdly, I am of the opinion that members of Western Region senior management, certainly Mr Lattimer, the Assistant General Manager, and probably, at least initially, Mr Ibbotson, the General Manager himself, were very much influenced by the Railway Inspectorate's drive to install AHB crossings and in particular they were well aware of the Inspectorate's use of the Welsh Marches line as a testing ground for running trains non-stop at high average speeds between the larger stations (Ibbotson was also a former Royal Engineers lieutenant-colonel). Moreover, Western Region funded T. A. Matthews, a firm of Herefordshire solicitors, to act as legal agents, to conduct a special campaign of prosecuting as many errant vehicle drivers as they could for supposedly poor and dangerous conduct, at one crossing in particular: Leominster, Kington junction. The crossing was watched over by an attendant, from its conversion in October 1966 until the end of September 1967, three times the usual time span.

Fourthly, there was a disagreement between parts of the Ministry of Transport concerning the siting and orientation of the dual-purpose 'IN EMERGENCY – PHONE SIGNALMAN' signboard, which on the balance of probabilities was the major causal factor of the Hixon disaster. In brief, Mr Alexander, the senior man from the Roads Engineering Department, realized the signboard should be sited facing oncoming road traffic, if the lower-case message relating the need for drivers of exceptional or heavy loads to phone the signalman before attempting to cross was to stand any chance at all of being effective. He told the S&T technicians at Hixon that the signboards should be located 'more facing the road'. Which is of course open to two interpretations! Suffice to say that there is good reason to believe that the angle of the signboards was altered at least once in between the conversion to AHB working and the accident. Added to this we have the fact that Colonel Reed considered the upper-case message to be more important, and had said so both in correspondence with British Railways and almost certainly, but of course impossible to prove, in conversation with the S&T inspectors at Hixon, who were responsible for erecting the signboards.

Moreover, the installation blueprint for the Hixon crossing clearly shows the two dual-purpose signboards to be at a very narrow angle to the carriageway, approximately 11° or 12°; that is, virtually parallel. There is interesting photographic evidence from up and down the country in newspaper reports at the time, that clearly show how the S&T technicians in various locations had angled the signboard differently: some parallel, as at Birkdale near Southport, some face on to the carriageway, as at Pontsarn in South Wales. The instructions were ambiguous, and not surprisingly were interpreted differently at different crossings . How Chairman Gibbens reconciled this issue, in a most remarkable way with regard to Hixon crossing, is dealt with in chapter 8.

Finally, having traced his long-ago doings regarding AHB installation in detail over the past five years or so, I feel impelled to present the 'pursuit' of Colonel Reed during the Hixon Inquiry hearings. There are two reasons for this: first, because of all the seven Ministry of Transport witnesses, Reed is by far the most interesting, largely because he is the only one who doesn't abide entirely by the plan imposed by Under-Secretary Scott-Malden (which can be summarized as: 'We've 'fessed up to collective, partial responsibility; if we all stay on message and look contrite, we'll be okay.'). As he makes clear time and again, Reed did not believe he was responsible in the slightest for the Hixon disaster. The second reason for my particular interest in Reed, is that my researches for this book have convinced me that he was in fact pre-eminently responsible for the circumstances that brought about not only Hixon, but also the Beckingham accident of 16 April 1968.

So why did Colonel Reed deny, under oath, that he had been told of the events at Leominster of 8 November 1966 in late February of 1967? It only takes a little thought to realize the implications if it had been established that Reed had known about what Chairman Gibbens described as the 'near catastrophe at Leominster' ten months before the Hixon collision and then done nothing. In that event, in the context of the Hixon Inquiry, the sky would have fallen in on him and the rest of the Railway Inspectorate. Reed had to deny any knowledge, or be prepared to take the consequences, and quite clearly he was not ready to do that. Strangely, in a way it was a relatively safe line to take because it was purely Reed's word against the then Movements Manager for British Railways' Western Region, Mr Brennan. Because of course, the Railway Inspectorate had never been officially informed of the events at Leominster; Brennan had not put pen to paper, presumably thinking that he was dealing with a person of integrity in Colonel Reed. Also, to be absolutely fair to him, Reed might genuinely have forgotten the encounter, although that seems extraordinary, given that he was being informed of a serious incident at a crossing, that he then went on to recommend as fit for use. Yet again with Reed, one is driven to the conclusion that his mind was shut to any criticism of AHB crossings or their installation process; the only problems he was inclined to acknowledge were to do with the supposed ill-disciplined behaviour of the motorists who were using them. If Reed had had an open mind about AHB crossings, then he would have done what he and his Inspectorate colleagues had successfully accomplished on many occasions over many years: carry out an expeditious investigation into the facts, and then act upon the findings.

Why he did not do this has already been touched upon: the Inspectorate were not acting impartially or indeed rationally as far as AHB installations were concerned. They had concluded that the new crossings were safe under virtually all circumstances and therefore must be protected from any 'unjustified' criticism; moreover, anything which might be interpreted as being even slightly negative in its tone regarding the innovative technology was to be suppressed.

Certainly, the *Hixon Inquiry Report* castigates the directors of Wynns for failing to make the link between a stationary level-crossing blocking hazard and a slowly moving level-crossing blocking hazard, stating that, 'The two hazards are not very different in kind.' The report then goes on to identify as the 'principal factor' behind the Hixon collision, the further failure of the directors of Wynns to extrapolate from this similarity between the stationary and the slowly moving hazard, to the extent that they should have gone on to 'discover the proper procedure for their heavy vehicles when using automatic crossings and to instruct their drivers accordingly'. Wynns' directors were, at worst, somewhat remiss in not making those two links (especially going on to 'discover the proper procedures' etc.) and had indeed admitted as much, but their admission would have faded into insignificance had it emerged that the principal architect of the AHB crossings' installation programme, Colonel Reed, had apparently had drawn to his attention a full ten months before the Hixon collision the exact same similarity of hazard, and who had then done nothing. Reed maintained throughout his evidence to the Hixon Inquiry that he had never considered the possibility of a slowly moving abnormal load blocking one of his beloved AHB crossings.

It is difficult not to agree with the logic of the expert witness, Professor Colin Buchanan, that the possibility of a train-wrecking obstruction on one of the new crossings could never have been considered by the senior personnel responsible for AHB introduction, prior to the Hixon collision, or they would surely have taken steps to ensure that such an occurrence could not happen. In the *Hixon Inquiry Report* itself it is concluded that the issue of a slowly moving, or stationary, level-crossing blocking and therefore train-wrecking obstruction was recognized only dimly in the minds of those responsible senior personnel in the Ministry of Transport. This would certainly have been very far from the truth, if one of them, Colonel Reed, had been told of the Leominster incident of 8 November 1966, in late February of 1967, and had either forgotten about it, or else had disregarded the information. Both of these circumstances would amount to gross negligence for someone in Reed's position. Quite why Mr Brennan or indeed Leslie Lloyd were not summoned to the inquiry to put their assertions in person to Reed is puzzling. One of the cross-examining barristers, ended up brandishing Lloyd's witness statement in front of Reed, saying, 'You have read this, have you Colonel Reed?'

Wading through forty-nine-year-old inquiry papers can be somewhat tedious, although occasionally you do get an interesting chunk of genuine legal drama. The verbal duels between Colonel Reed and two eminent barristers, Mr Blennerhassett for the Inquiry and Mr Fay for British Railways, certainly fall into this category, but in the end, by sticking to his steadfast denial of knowledge of any crossing blocking incident at Leominster prior to Hixon, Reed was triumphant (Barristers 0, Reed 1). The two barristers also quizzed him about his role in the design and siting of the 'IN EMERGENCY – PHONE SIGNALMAN' signboard, both generally and also specifically, as to how it was placed at Hixon crossing. First off , Reed agreed that he had overruled a suggestion from British Railways S&T Department that two separate signs were necessary in the circumstances; then referring to Hixon in particular he cheerfully admitted that he would have approved it facing parallel to the road as far as his personal preference was concerned, although he stressed he was not asserting that was how it had actually been sited on the day of the collision, and he made it clear he was not speaking on behalf of the Ministry. (That is amazing 'brass-neck' and Mr Scott-Malden, if he was observing the proceedings, which he usually was, must have been far from happy.) At the same time Reed argued that there was no evidence to show that the signboard with its dual message was not adequate, his logic being that there had only been one 'Hixon' and therefore it must have been fine on numerous other occasions. He seems to have overreached himself here, because Chairman Gibbens was not persuaded, pointing out that the two signalmen at Colwich signal-box had reported receiving only one call from the crossing in six months from the police escort of a similar vehicle to the Wynns' juggernaut, whereas it was documented that six such 'exceptional' vehicles had used the crossing in that time (five of Wynns and one of Pickfords). Although Reed was quite happy to defend the signboard, up to a point, he was reluctant to have the design put down to him, even though he seemed to be splitting hairs here, in that he admitted he had overseen and approved the dual design, but that he believed the actual design had been suggested by another part of the Ministry of Transport. From this Chairman Gibbens concluded in his report (paragraph 188) that the design of the signboard came from the Traffic Engineering Division in the Ministry, even though he states, there had been no evidence to that effect offered by that division. (Not offering evidence, in this context, *can* indicate that one party may not agree with something another party has said, but does not want to 'rock the boat'.) This is no small point, because as well as the dual-purpose design of the signboard, it was at this stage (early in 1964) that the word 'heavy' appears for the first time on the signboard, so that the lower-case message read, 'or before crossing with exceptional or *heavy* loads or cattle'. Somebody had thought about the likelihood of something other than combine harvesters using the crossings; was it Colonel Reed? What looked like his handwriting appeared in the margin of the correspondence specifying the changes in design (two sizes of lettering) and wording ('heavy' to be inserted) that he wanted. He denied it was his, saying it belonged to his clerical assistant. Anyway, at this juncture, Reed was saved from further questioning by the split nature of the Inquiry: the signboard design was deemed by Chairman Gibbens to be a policy matter, which was to be dealt with by Colonel McMullen. (This time it was Barristers 2, Reed 0 – but with the ref allowing a substitute.)

Gibbens makes the point in his report that it would be unreasonable to expect the officers of the Ministry of Transport to remember every jot and tittle of their decisions and procedures relating to AHB installation, because some of these would inevitably fall through the bureaucratic 'interstices' of the Ministry's workings. However, when there was, first, what was on the face of it, such a precise and overwhelmingly important question regarding Reed's state of knowledge of a blocked level-crossing incident prior to Hixon to be examined, surely Gibbens should have insisted upon Lloyd or Brennan being summoned? Moreover, the split nature of the Inquiry seems to have worked very clearly against establishing who was responsible for the design of the inadequate signboard that was at the root of the Hixon disaster. (Mr Scott-Malden in a note he made, described Gibbens's intervention, ruling that Reed should not be questioned any further, as 'most helpful.')

One broad assumption that Chairman Gibbens makes about the Inspectorate is that they were, as he puts it, only 'dimly' aware of the large, slowly moving indivisible load problem, from mid-1964 onwards. There is no real evidence for this. What there is evidence for, because two members of the Inspectorate, Colonel McMullen and Major Olver (and Mr Scott-Malden), said so in their evidence, and Gibbens makes a point of mentioning in the report, with open incredulity (paragraph 187), is that they had never thought of a vehicle the size of those used by Wynns, or Pickfords, *at all.* Colonel Reed, on the other hand, had at the very least 'signed off' what he considered to be an adequate precautionary notice for drivers of 'exceptional or heavy loads'. That's not being 'dimly' aware of large, slowly moving, indivisible loads, unless, as one exasperated barrister put it, 'he was thinking of Traction Engines'. Moreover, from his cross-examination it is plain Reed considered at the time that he authorized the signboard that the more important part of it was the upper case 'IN EMERGENCY – PHONE SIGNALMAN', and that therefore the S&T personnel installing the signboards would have been doing so in accordance with his expectations, if they had put them in parallel to the carriageway and sited close to the barriers. It is worth reiterating that the blueprint for the Hixon AHB crossing clearly has the signboard close to the barriers and at an angle of approximately 12° to the carriageway, that is virtually parallel. Not only did Reed continue to stress in his evidence that he thought the dual-purpose signboard perfectly adequate, but he revealed that *after* the Hixon accident at Hixon crossing itself, once it had been put back together, he arranged for the 'IN EMERGENCY' signboards to be erected at an angle of 12° to the carriageway, so that he could take photographs to demonstrate just how adequate they were. This evidence was given towards the end of the first part of the hearings, on the Hixon accident itself, on the 23rd day to be precise, so nothing Reed had heard caused him to change his mind about the signboard. Perhaps not surprisingly, on the same day Chairman Gibbens said he 'was sorry to hear Colonel Reed' still maintaining that it was allowable to install AHB crossings without taking any regard of their individual traffic peculiarities, such as the English Electric depot at Hixon (paragraph 176 of the *Hixon Inquiry Report*).

Chapter 7

Tragedy at Trent Road level-crossing, Beckingham, Lincolnshire: Tuesday, 16 April 1968

Colonel Denis McMullen was the thirteenth Chief Inspecting Officer (CIO) of Railways, since the position had been established in1840; by the time he had formulated his initial response for the Hixon Inquiry he may well have been wondering if he would be the last. It is worth noting that McMullen very carefully distances himself from the day-to-day work on AHB crossing installation, although he acknowledges that he was responsible for formally 'signing off' each conversion. However, prior to taking up the post of CIO in 1963 following the retirement of Brigadier C. A. Langley, McMullen had been very closely involved with the installation of AHBs from the mid-fifties through to late 1961, when automation of level-crossings was made the responsibility of one inspector: Colonel Reed. Up to this point progress in installing automatic crossings had been glacial, with only two in use by the end of 1961.The reason behind this was clear: the guidelines contained in 'The Provisional Requirements of the Minister of Transport ... in Regard to Automatically Operated Half-Barriers at Public Level Crossings', published in 1958, were too restrictive; in brief, installation would only be permitted where the speed of trains did not exceed 60 mph and the daily total of motor vehicle movements at a crossing did not exceed a thousand.

Colonel McMullen had again gone abroad, in 1961, this time to the USA and Canada and concluded that:

> we might consider relaxing some of our requirements ... On the other hand, I am convinced that before this equipment can be used on fast running lines, we must adopt some system of measuring the speed of trains ... to avoid an unduly long period of time elapsing after [the barriers] have fallen and before the arrival of a slow train.

From this it is clear that McMullen still harboured doubts about train controlled crossings in their purest and simplest form. His colleague Colonel Reed of course had fewer such doubts, and he was the one in day-to-day charge of AHB crossing installation. In particular the issue of 'measuring the speed of trains' and consequently introducing differentiation between slow and fast trains, as to how quickly the barriers fell when a train activated a crossing mechanism, was never prioritized. Although around this time at Leominster (confirmed by Phil Jones) on the Up line in particular, extra treadles were tested and provided, to cope with the perceived problem of trains starting off from a standstill at the station, and therefore taking an inordinate amount of time before they ran onto the nearby level-crossing, with its ever impatient motorists waiting at the barriers. There exists a draft letter that Colonel Reed wrote at the time he recommended the Leominster crossing for commissioning in early 1967, in it he raises concerns about the fact that this speed differentiation work was taking place, he felt that the waiting time for motorists was potentially being *increased* too much. As ever Reed wanted to keep things as simple as possible. What is interesting about this unsent letter is that it reveals Reed was not the one overseeing the speed differentiation work, that therefore would have been authorised by the S&T Department management, that is John Tyler.

So some work was being done on the problem of differentiation between slow and fast trains, but it was focused on the issue that McMullen had identified, which was that of motorists having to wait longer if a train was travelling slowly, and being thus tempted to zigzag around the barriers. Neither McMullen or Reed, or anybody else who was specifying AHB crossing design, ever considered the mirror image of this, a train arriving on a crossing unusually rapidly. As a result, the 'critical second train situation' was an accident risk that was never fully appreciated by the Inspectorate. Although it was known that the supposed minimum twenty-four-second gap between a train 'striking in' and its arrival on the crossing, could be reduced to as little as sixteen to eighteen seconds in some predictable circumstances, and one of those 'predictable circumstances' was about to manifest itself.

The other fatal level-crossing accident that occurred in 1968 and that justifiably receives a great deal of attention in the *Hixon Inquiry Report*, is the collision between an express passenger train and a family saloon car, at Trent Road level-crossing, Beckingham, in Lincolnshire. This resulted in five deaths, three of them being those of young children. The details of this accident are still extremely distressing, even at a distance in time of nearly fifty years. It also fits neatly, and chillingly, into the category of the 'acceptable' accident, identified by Professor Colin Buchanan, the kind of thing the proponents of AHB crossings were apparently prepared to tolerate, as the occasional result of their introduction of automatic level-crossings onto the railway network. The Beckingham accident happened on the Tuesday after Easter Monday, whereas on Easter Monday itself, a bizarre incident occurred at Yapton AHB crossing on the Southern Region: a Ford Anglia two-door saloon with a driver and three passengers was following close behind another car towing a dinghy on a trailer; the first car came to a brief halt on the crossing, which caused the Anglia driver to brake and then stall the engine which would not restart, leaving his car obstructing both railway lines. The crossing lights flashed and the bells jangled and down came the barriers, upon which the occupants of the Anglia got out and got clear. There were two trains (both electrical multiple units) approaching the crossing from either direction; they had both passed the last signals that could have arrested their progress. However, the drivers of each of the approaching trains spotted the obstruction in front of them and applied the brakes, and as a result each train came to a halt, one forty yards away and the other only five yards away from the car. Both drivers then got down from their trains and helped to push the offending Anglia off the crossing. In a way this almost comic incident helps to explain how the public, and ordinary railway personnel, were learning fast as to how to cope with the AHB hazard: that is, the train drivers were probably not sticking to instructions to approach the crossings at maximum operating speed, thereby giving themselves more of a chance of stopping at a blocked crossing, and members of the public were beginning to realize that the only thing to be done if your car was stuck on a crossing, was to get clear, and quickly. (We also have the example of Mr Stuart, the train driver on the Welsh Marches line, who said in his letter to the Hixon Inquiry that he always approached Leominster AHB crossing in particular at 75 mph instead of the prescribed 90 mph.)

Prior to examining the circumstances of the Beckingham accident itself, it is worth looking at how it was handled by the Hixon Inquiry. Because on the face of it, this collision was just what those in overall charge of the inquiry at the Ministry of Transport would have been dreading: another AHB crossing calamity with multiple fatalities, before they were able to receive a considered judgement on Hixon itself, and how to prevent it happening again. In effect, 'it', or something very similar had now happened again. Given that the Hixon Inquiry's broader remit was to look at all aspects of the introduction of automatic level-crossings, this further accident should surely have been investigated as a priority by Chairman Gibbens and his team of assessors? Instead this task was to be 'given back' to the Railway Inspectorate, in the person of Colonel J. R. H. Robertson, an experienced Inspector, who, fortuitously, had played no direct part in the introduction of AHB crossings.

Again, on the face of it, this outcome should have been exactly what the senior officials in the Railways Group at the Ministry most desired: investigation of an AHB accident back in the hands of the Railway Inspectorate. Not a bit of it! The Secretary of the Hixon Inquiry, W. Patrick Jackson had seized the moment and drafted a letter for the Minister of Transport, to appoint Colonel Robertson to produce a limited factual report, as soon as possible, to be fed directly into the Hixon Inquiry. Robertson was appointed on the very same day that the Beckingham accident took place, by a new Minister of Transport. Prime Minister Harold Wilson had carried out a ministerial reshuffle: Barbara Castle had been made Secretary of State for Employment and Productivity, replaced at Transport by Richard Marsh MP, who had technically been in his new post for ten days, since 6 April, but who had only carried out his first official duty on Easter Monday, 15 April, when he had appeared on the TV news urging people to wear seatbelts in their cars. In his 1978 autobiography, *Off the Rails*, Marsh states he had neither expected or wanted to become Minister of Transport, a subject area for which he said he had 'no experience or indeed inclination', which, given his later five-year stint as Chairman of British Railways, is amusing, to say the least.

The PM's decision to put Marsh into place was apparently based on a wish to have somebody who was 'media-savvy' heading up the complex Transport brief, and despite Marsh's own initial reservations, this appears to have been a typically shrewd and effective move by Wilson. Marsh's autobiography further reveals that he did not start work at his desk in his new Ministry until after the Easter break was over, which means that his rapid appointment of Robertson on 16 April to report on the Beckingham incident, would have been one of his very first actions as minister. This seems at the least, to demonstrate an intention to take decisive action, or possibly more accurately to be seen to be taking decisive action. Because, of course, since the Hixon collision, Fleet Street had, not unnaturally, taken a very keen interest in anything and everything to do with automatic level-crossings, and on Wednesday, 17 April, the national dailies all featured the tragic details of what had happened the previous day at Trent Road level-crossing, together with coverage of the Yapton incident. Added to which, there was a growing catalogue of reports of further near-misses and worrying occurrences relating to the 'robot' crossings, from up and down the country.

Colonel Robertson completed his investigation and published his report on 3 May, less than three weeks after the accident. Robertson states as his main finding that the cause of an accident that cost five lives, was the stalling of a car (an Austin A40 saloon) on a level-crossing with a 60 mph express train only eighteen seconds away. Having been told to stick to the facts of the matter, he makes no attempt to analyze how that situation had been allowed to arise. *The Times* front page report from 17 April describes the final moments before the impact: 'Mr John Hilton, got out and tried to push the car containing his three children and his mother-in-law to safety. Although he could have leapt aside at the last moment, he died in the crash with his children.'

It is this accident, more so even than the Hixon accident itself, that makes the blood run cold, particularly if one can recall driving motor vehicles of thirty or forty years ago, with engines which, once stalled, did not instantaneously spring back into life at the first turn of the ignition key, as most modern cars do. The fact is that Mr Hilton was not acting in a reckless or unusual manner: he was merely trying to get from one side of the crossing to the other, and he stalled his car in the path of an oncoming train, almost certainly as a result of the half-barrier across on the other carriageway coming down, not directly in front of him but within his field of vision and thereby startling him. He was the first in a queue at the level-crossing, having pulled up in front of a lowered barrier. A goods train travelling at around 40 mph passed by and the barrier lifted, Mr Hilton moved his car forward onto the crossing and as he was part way across, the lights began to flash again and the barriers to fall; he stalled and having failed to restart the engine, he tried to push the car laden with his family out of harm's way. But to no avail. According to one eye-witness, his desperate efforts only succeeded in shifting it forward by about a foot; when he got out of his car, the express was a mere six seconds away. This 'critical second train situation' had arisen because, after the first train, the goods, had 'struck out', the barriers had taken around six seconds to rise to their open position. *At the same time*, as the goods struck out, the express coming in the other direction 'struck in', and because the flashing lights and bells could not commence working until the barriers were fully upright, this had the effect of reducing the normal twenty-four-second warning to around eighteen seconds.

Chairman Gibbens of the Hixon Inquiry does not seek to conceal his concern about Colonel Robertson's report, particularly because it enabled him to point up the so-called 'critical second train situation' as being totally unacceptable as things stood. Unlike at Hixon, there was no doubt at all who was at fault here: the Inspectorate had specified much too short a time span before a second train appeared on a crossing, particularly as motorists would be moving forward from being stationary, and were therefore more likely to stall. It was essential that the situation should be remedied, and the only way to do so was to provide an additional twenty-second warning period if a second train was close; doing this required additional strike-in treadles, fifty-two seconds away from the crossing. For high-speed operation that meant locating the treadles (one on each line) around 2,500 yards away from the crossing. Nationwide, that meant an awful lot of extra copper wire cabling to connect the treadles to the crossings, for the Railway to pay for.

Don't forget this undeniably necessary 'second train' modification came before any other recommendations that Gibbens had in mind for increased treadle distances, to give a slightly longer waiting time, for those ever impatient motorists behind the half-barriers.

Chapter 8

The mind of a Judge
(and the cost of copper wire)

What considerations were in the Chairman of the Hixon Inquiry's mind when he came to write up his findings once all of the evidence was in, and the last witness had been cross-examined? The final day of the hearings was on Wednesday, 29 May 1968. The report was published, only just over a month later on Monday, 1 July. Compared with the time taken by more recent public inquiries to issue their findings, this seems phenomenally quick work; but then Chairman Gibbens knew he had to get his findings and recommendations into the public domain, and more importantly into action on the rail network, as rapidly as possible. (The letter he had received from Transport Minister Richard Marsh after the Beckingham accident had urged a speedy completion of the report because of the huge public disquiet there was regarding the 200 or so AHB crossings scattered across the country, like so many unexploded bombs. (One wonders if Patrick Jackson, the Secretary to the Inquiry, told Gibbens that Marsh's letter had in fact been written by him!)

Fortunately for Gibbens as well as the excellent Jackson he had very good technical support as to the changes that needed to be made for the safer functioning of the AHB crossings that were in operation. The hand of Professor Colin Buchanan can be seen in the four most important changes that were made: firstly, the time between a train striking in to a treadle mechanism and appearing on the crossing was extended from a scant twenty-four seconds to a minimum of thirty-five seconds for even the fastest trains. This was to be achieved by placing the treadles further away from the crossings. (Also, one of British Railways Regions, Southern, had operated just with track circuits being 'shorted out' to trigger the crossings' mechanisms. The report advised that the treadle system should be introduced to Southern as well).

Secondly, the murderously short time span, just sixteen to eighteen seconds, that had been possible as far as the 'critical second train' situation was concerned was adjusted to thirty seconds.

Thirdly, the issue of signage was addressed, as a matter of urgency, and even before the report was published the dual-purpose 'IN EMERGENCY – PHONE SIGNALMAN' signboard was replaced across the country by two separate signboards, correctly placed and oriented for their intended audiences. This was brought about by a direct request from the Hixon Inquiry to British

Railways, with no consultation with the Railway Inspectorate. (The separation of the two messages had already been in place at Leominster AHB crossing since the autumn of 1966 (*see* plate 2). There is also evidence that other innovations in signage had taken place prior to the Hixon accident at Leominster, under the direction of Mr Alexander of the Ministry of Transport's Road Engineering Division and against the wishes of the Railway Inspectorate, that is, Colonel Reed. This came out in the cross-examination of Mr Hale of the Ministry's Road Signs Division, who revealed that because Leominster crossing was on a trunk road any signage there, was the direct responsibility of Alexander, who had had put in 'Level-crossing Ahead: Automatic Barriers' signboards on the approaches to the crossing.)

Looking to the future, the treatment of the design of the approach to an automatic level-crossing, by assuming it to be the first experience that a motorist would have of one, and furthermore assuming no prior knowledge whatsoever, was recommended as the only appropriate way forward. Finally, all AHB crossings were to be equipped with telephones placed in or close to the barriers, for the use of the public in emergency situations, and there were to be more telephones placed at an appropriate distance on either side of the crossing for routine non-emergency use by lorry drivers and farmers.

As far as the Railway Inspectorate / Railways Group of the Ministry of Transport, were concerned they were thanked in the report for their trouble in providing the inquiry with a lengthy document detailing what they considered to be the options as to the future of AHB crossings. However, Chairman Gibbens made it perfectly clear that whilst he was aware of their opinions, he felt under no obligation to take any notice of them. The essential thing had been accomplished: the responsibility for implementing Gibbens's recommendations was now firmly and unambiguously in the hands of British Railways.

These wider findings and recommendations of the report were implemented quickly, just as the Minister, Richard Marsh, wanted; however, they were not universally welcomed by any means. Even one of Gibbens's two assessors, the signage and street lighting expert, Granville Berry, had declined to put his name to the report's recommendations regarding retaining partial protection only for AHB crossings. In adopting this position Berry was agreeing with the view expressed during the inquiry by John Tyler, the Chief S&T Engineer, on behalf of British Railways, that partial protection was 'wrong in principle'. However, Tyler had gone on to say that if partial protection was decided by the Inquiry, British Railways 'would have to accept it, but we do not like it'.

There are two main reasons Gibbens had decided upon retaining AHB crossings essentially as they were (although incorporating the changes outlined above) firstly, and undoubtedly carrying huge weight (particularly with the Government) was the fact that restoring full-blown signal interlocking protection would have been ruinously expensive; and moreover would have largely destroyed the savings in time for motorists waiting at the barriers, that AHB crossings provided. Secondly, Professor Colin Buchanan had given as his opinion, that although the old, fully gated, signal-interlocked and manned crossings, were marginally safer than AHBs ('they just about shave it'), this did not outweigh the advantages of automation. This was good enough for Gibbens, who advised British Railways to press on rapidly and install many more automatic crossings, adopting the changes he had specified, of course. And therein lay the major difficulty with implementing his recommendations: even with retaining AHB crossings, the cost of the extra copper wire that was required to link up all the necessary new switch treadles was huge. Despite his urging them to set about converting as many more level-crossings as possible, the rate of progress was slow; by 1978 only another thirty-three crossings had been turned over to AHB working by British Railways, whereas at the time of the Hixon disaster it had been widely reported in the press that British Railways intended to provide another 1,300 AHB crossings.

In more recent years there has been a concerted move towards replacing each AHB crossing, that is thought suitable, with a bridge. Hixon crossing itself, was 'done away with', to use Colonel Reed's felicitous phrase, in this fashion in 2002. Which mention of Hixon, brings us back around to the primary reason Brian Gibbens was asked to chair his inquiry and produce his report.

Gibbens could certainly be forgiven if he considered that he had got the easier part of his remit out of the way, in his decisions on the future of all automatic crossings in this country. As to deciding, definitively, what had occurred at only one of them in the recent past, that was a much more sensitive and demanding task. In particular Gibbens had to make a choice as to who to believe on one apparently, overwhelmingly important issue regarding Hixon: that is, which way was the dual-purpose 'IN EMERGENCY – PHONE SIGNALMAN' signboard, facing on Saturday, 6 January 1968? Was it facing approaching traffic, or was it sideways on (parallel) to the carriageway? This signboard was the one that gave the vital information regarding the need to phone the signalman for 'exceptional vehicles' approaching from the direction of the A51, and it was the only surviving signboard, its twin having been swept away by the encroaching wreckage of the locomotive and the first six carriages of the express, together with the former crossing keeper's hut, with its phone. Gibbens commented in his report that the matter of the precise position of the signboard had been extensively reported on in the press, and that it had been said that the reason why neither the crew of the transporter nor the police escort saw it 'was that it was parallel to the road [in which position it was certainly found immediately after the accident] so that no approaching driver would either see or read it' (paragraph 148).

Gibbens decided to settle the matter by using that trusty tool of lawyers in a hurry, the 'legal fiction' – *a presumption of fact assumed by a court for convenience, consistency, or to achieve justice* – and ruled that the signboard was facing approaching traffic at an angle of approximately 26°, that is, more or less, facing oncoming traffic. This ruling he made 'with some certainty' based on the evidence of the analysis of two photographs of the crossing carried out by Flight Lieutenant R. D. Moreau, an RAF photo-reconnaissance analyst, on behalf of the inquiry. The Inquiry was told that the two photographs were taken, one on Friday, 8 December 1967 and the other on Saturday, 16 December 1967, by 'a keen young amateur photographer, Mr Iain Campbell'. Mr Campbell had read of the conflict of evidence in the press, and had approached, the Ministry of Transport who had eventually referred him to the Inquiry. The two photographs both show the dual-purpose signboard, clearly visible and readable from the road approaching the crossing, just as a motorist would see them. Moreover, one image conveniently shows lying snow, which was recorded as occurring at Hixon crossing on 8 December … so of course, that must have been when it was taken. Flight Lieutenant Moreau gave no written proof of evidence, and he was only in front of the Inquiry for a scant five minutes at most, and departed without any cross-examination. Moreau's comments were confined entirely to giving his expert opinion of the angle of the signboard, as it appeared on the images that had been given to him for analysis. Chairman Gibbens said at the time he gave his evidence: 'The odd thing is there are a number of witnesses who have said when shown Mr Campbell's photographs that it [the signboard] was never in that position' [26 degrees] However this scepticism had disappeared by the time he wrote the Report, when Gibbens stated that although the signboard had been found after the collision to be in the 'sideways on' position – at an angle of 12° to the carriageway, the *precise* angle specified in the crossing's installation blueprint (*see* plate 21) – it 'had very probably been displaced by rescuers pushing past it after the crash'. It must be said that the case for the angle of the signboard being returned to its exact blueprint position, after the collision, by being pushed past seems fanciful in the extreme: it was seven feet off the ground, protected by a stout fence from access from the roadway, and fixed securely to a metal post with metal bands. What gave the suggestion of rescuers accidentally altering the angle of the sign some credence, at least in the mind of Chairman Gibbens, was that a small section of fence had been removed to allow extra access onto the tracks at some point during the rescue operation. There is a photograph that *must* have been taken on the Saturday afternoon because it appears in the *Sunday Mirror* of 7 January and it clearly shows the slight bend in the post, but also that the signboard itself is at an angle of 12° to the carriageway. Therefore, if the signboard *had* been moved from its purported angle of around 26° then this must have been done on the Saturday afternoon.

Moreover, we know that Mr Mackmurdie, British Railways' Divisional Supervisor, had admitted that he had tried at around 6.30 on the evening of the disaster to see if the sign was loose, 'with one hand', and had failed to budge it; furthermore, we know that the two *Birmingham Post* journalists, Thompson and Hill, had put in an evidential statement to the Inquiry that they had seen someone attempting to shift the signboard, 'wrestling with it' around noon on Sunday the 7th. Mackmurdie denied that it was him on the Sunday and could offer no suggestion as to who it might have been. (As can be seen from plates 19 and 20 that were taken earlier that same morning, the metal post *is* bent over slightly, which would be consistent with someone pulling and pushing with enough force on it. Could it have been the same unidentified person on the Saturday afternoon, who then came back for another try on the Sunday morning?)

So, what on earth was Gibbens up to ruling with such certainty that the signboard was definitely facing the carriageway at the time of the collision? The answer to that, is that it *might* conceivably have been facing the carriageway, and extrapolating from that, that it *was* so angled, gave Gibbens the opportunity to put one or two people in their place, as it were, when he came to write up his report, specifically, the Chief Constable of Staffordshire, Arthur Rees, and Colin Parsons, the 'statutory attendant' in Wynns' forward tractor, both of whom had irked Gibbens in their evidence-giving to the Inquiry; and in the case of Rees by his use of the *Birmingham Post* and its sister title, *Sunday Mail* to get his version of what position the dual-purpose signboard was in at Hixon crossing, into the public domain very early and effectively.

Not any more it wasn't ! As far as the report was concerned the chairman had the last word as to which position the signboard was in; it was his report after all and he clearly was not going to have any aspect of it pre-empted by anybody else. The question of real importance that Gibbens had to come to a judgement on, relating to the Hixon signboard, was not whether anybody in the Wynns' forward tractor crew or their police escort had seen it, read it, understood it and then ignored it, all four men had stated that they had not seen the signboard until after the collision. Rather, Gibbens had to ask who could reasonably have been expected to see it, read it and act upon what they had seen? In the end, Gibbens concluded that the two policemen, PC Prince and PC Nicholls, had not seen the signboard as they drove past at normal speed, and even if they had seen it, in those circumstances they would not have been able to read the lower-case message 'or before crossing with exceptional or heavy loads or cattle' which applied to them. Gibbens then went on to criticize them for 'failing to consider intelligently whether such a vehicle [as they were escorting] could safely cross the railway, and to make inquiries'. But crucially he ruled that 'They had not observed the Emergency Notice' (and could not therefore have been expected to act upon it). (Finding 3, page 115.)

Turning to Bryn Groves and Colin Parsons, the crew of the forward tractor. Gibbens in Finding 1 says this: 'the driver of a huge transporter vehicle failed to comply with a notice erected near the stop line on the approach road directing him to telephone the signalman before attempting to cross.' The key phrase here, of course, is 'failed to comply'. Now, whereas ignorance of the law is no excuse, ignorance of a fact, such as an instruction, is, or can be. The emergency notice was not a lawful road sign: it had about the same status in law as that of a 'Trespassers will be Prosecuted' sign. Gibbens goes on in Finding 2 to say this: 'The driver of the transporter, Mr B. H. Groves, did not know of the existence of such a notice nor of the need to telephone for permission to cross the line, but he or his statutory attendant, Mr R. C. Parsons, ought to have seen it and complied with it.' So, Gibbens concludes, they had not seen the signboard, even though they 'ought to have'. Again, if they did not see it, in law, they cannot have been expected to act upon it.

With these findings, Gibbens to a great extent protects the two policemen and the two Wynns' employees from any possibility of additional criminal proceedings being brought against them. (Although he does single out Colin Parsons for stating in his evidence that he did not think it was part of his job to look out for road signs or notices, Gibbens quotes the relevant legislation at him, pointing out that it *was* part of his job, and stating that: 'Consequently, he did not observe the Emergency Notice, as he should have done.' (Paragraph 102.)) Whether Gibbens *intended* to protect the four men at the scene from possible criminal prosecution is impossible to say but that was the effect of his findings as far as their actions were concerned.

As a Judge, Gibbens was used to making similar judgements as to culpability in both civil and criminal cases, the level of proof necessary in criminal cases being the strict 'beyond reasonable doubt' versus the more inclusive 'on the balance of probabilities' test used for civil cases. Of course, the Inquiry was not being held under the criminal law; however, what Gibbens would have been very aware of, was that his rulings and recommendations could be used to trigger criminal proceedings, if the evidential basis for such proceedings seemed clear enough. The Railway Inspectorate were well aware of the possibility of such occurrences: quite often in the past their investigations had resulted in railwaymen standing trial on criminal charges, the most recent of note being after the Southall accident and investigation of 1959, when one of the train drivers involved had been put on trial for manslaughter, twice, and acquitted both times. (Later on, it had emerged that a design fault in the forward-facing observation window of his 'Battle of Britain' class locomotive made it virtually certain that he had been telling the truth, when he said he had not seen a red signal.)

Having dealt with the Wynns' crew and their police escort as to how they had lamentably, but not deliberately, failed to negotiate the conditions at Hixon crossing on 6 January 1968, Gibbens ought then to have concentrated on identifying those who were responsible for putting those conditions into place, and gone as far back down the tree of causality as possible. This was the *sine qua non* approach that had been taken by the Aberfan Tribunal just over a year previously: the senior management of the National Coal Board were found to be at fault for having a policy of tipping thousands of tons of colliery waste onto steep hillsides over the top of streams and springs, not the colliery workers who tipped the waste, or even the middle managers who, ineptly, administered the tipping. The policy was wrong and disaster was judged to be inevitable. Similarly, with the Hixon Inquiry it had been established that the Ministry of Transport was pre-eminently responsible for installing AHB crossings with inadequate signage together with not distributing adequate publicity generally, and in particular not properly briefing the police or the road haulage industry, as to the revolutionary nature of the new crossings' mode of working. Disaster, somewhere, at some time, was therefore inevitable.

Instead of adopting the *sine qua non* approach of looking as far down the tree of causality as it was possible to go, Gibbens seized upon the fact that Wynns' directors had already admitted they should have 'done more to pursue the matter' when they received Lattimer's peculiar letter of response concerning the Leominster incident of 8 November 1966. As a result of this, Wynns were awarded the primary culpability 'for failing to discover the proper procedure for their heavy vehicles when using automatic crossings and to instruct their drivers accordingly'. This Gibbens identified as 'the principal factor contributing to the disaster'. As well as highlighting Wynns' response to the Leominster incident, Gibbens also suggests within the report (paragraph 117) that there were other sources of information that they 'might have noted' and which presumably might have alerted them to the danger AHB crossings posed to their operations: first, he observes that there was an AHB crossing installed at Pontsarn near Merthyr Tydfil, 'twenty miles from their headquarters at Newport' in April 1966. Now, this crossing was actually over forty miles away by road: although apparently close as the crow flies, it was quite remote to Wynns and their operations; also of course the attendant publicity for its installation had occurred eight months prior to the Leominster incident. Secondly, Gibbens states that paragraph 58 of the *Highway Code* provided information about AHB crossings, which it did, in general terms, but there is no mention of a telephone, still less of an essential telephone procedure for 'exceptional or heavy loads'.

Whilst not quite 'blaming the victims', Gibbens's placing of the shortcomings of Wynns' directors as 'the principal factor contributing to the disaster' does seem to be quite an eccentric decision. Especially as Wynns' transporter was travelling on a 'Special Order' route given to them by the Ministry of Transport, which route itinerary did not mention the Hixon crossing *at all*, never mind flagging up the absolute need to phone before crossing; although several bridges were mentioned as height hazards, so it gave the impression that the Ministry had assessed the route for places where extra caution was needed. The Ministry had taken a deliberate policy decision in 1966 not to mention the new AHB crossings in Special Order routes, because, after all, just like the old manned crossings, they were an obvious feature on a route. What the Ministry must have forgotten, of course, was that with the old crossings, it was still British Railways' responsibility to get vehicles safely from one side of the tracks to the other; now, with the AHB crossings, that imperative was with the road user, who if their vehicle constituted an 'exceptional or heavy load', needed to use the telephone, every time. (Gibbens also mentions Mr Preston (paragraph 127 of the *Hixon Inquiry Report*) the site manager for the English Electric company at the Hixon depot, who despite being unaware of the existence of the signboard advising of the need to phone, ought apparently to have advised Groves to phone the signalman before attempting to cross the lines. One is left wondering with Gibbens why he points up a supposed failing on the part of someone like Preston, who was really quite peripheral to matters at the crossing; it is as though he is casting about for as many people to share the blame amongst as possible.)

Next in order of culpability, according to Gibbens, were the Chief Constable and senior officers of Staffordshire Police who 'failed to instruct their constables about the working of automatic Crossings'. (Finding 5.) They had failed to do this because 'they had not read with care the Requirements and explanatory notes which were sent to them' two and a half years after the first AHB was put into Staffordshire and two and a half years before Hixon was converted. Gibbens gets himself in a bit of a pickle here as far as consistency is concerned, because in Finding 11 he states that the Ministry of Transport 'is responsible for the fact that the Chief Constable of Staffordshire was not properly briefed by the Home Office about the significant matters which would concern constables escorting heavy loads'. The reason for this lack of briefing was that the Home Office had received exactly the same 'Requirements and explanatory notes' that Staffordshire Police had … and concluded that they were of interest only to the Railway, as had Staffordshire Police before them. (The relevant piece of information that would have been useful to the two constables Prince and Nicholls, that is, the need to phone the signalman before attempting to cross with an exceptional load, was Requirement 18, which was six pages in to a pamphlet of what appeared to be technical instructions for the erection of AHBs. This was accompanied by an explanatory note which described the pamphlet of Requirements as 'an essential guide for the Railways when selecting sites'. There was no mention of any telephones in this note.)

A senior civil servant at the Home Office, Mr P. L. Taylor, gave evidence to the Inquiry in support of Chief Constable Rees, in which, in a few well-chosen words, he summed up the *sine qua non* approach: 'it was for the people who decide to set up a new system, whether … of dealing with drunken drivers, or with noisy cars or with gaming … or whatever it is, to have a clear idea of what they are expecting to happen, and they should let this be known to the people who have to carry out the actual work'. Taylor goes on to state the point that the Ministry of Transport, having brought AHB crossings into existence, clearly held the legal duty of properly briefing people like chief constables about them. (Now, it had already been established by the Inquiry that the full legal responsibility for getting their vehicles safely across the railway tracks at AHB crossings lay with ordinary motorists; *they* also were 'the people who have to carry out the actual work'. Surely a clever lawyer like Gibbens would have noticed that Taylor's words were applicable not just to chief constables but to the whole class of people: ordinary motorists, who now held the full legal responsibility for using automatic crossings safely.)

Gibbens agrees with, and adopts Taylor's comments (paragraph 217) but he does not seem to appreciate, or chooses to ignore, their potential usefulness as far as fairly apportioning culpability for the Hixon disaster was concerned. (Whereas the other Findings have some kind of logical progression, Finding 11, with its virtual negation of Finding 5's criticism of Chief Constable Rees, looks as though it has been added later, giving the impression that it has been 'crow-barred in' as the result of a hasty re-adjustment). It seems clear that Gibbens intended to publicly criticize Chief Constable Rees for being so openly dismissive of the Ministry of Transport's inept attempts to provide information about AHB crossings. Rees had said that he had no more knowledge of the working of AHB crossings than his two constables, Prince and Nicholls, 'which was very little'. Again, as with deciding what angle the dual-purpose signboard had been at, Gibbens clearly thought that it was his prerogative, not that of the Chief Constable, to state that the Ministry's 'attempt to convey information about the working of automatic crossing was inept', which, as it happens, he duly did in Finding 10.

Of course, by stating that he was no better informed than his two constables, the Chief Constable extended a kind of protection over them; late on the afternoon of the disaster, as they were helping with the rescue operation, he had brought the two men, individually, to the signboard, with its lower-case message of the need to telephone and asked them, 'Did you see this?'; horrified, both had immediately answered in the negative. Satisfied that they were telling the truth, he had then done his best to bring the inadequacies of the signboard to public attention. In short, he had stood by his men. (Rees was a former Welsh Rugby Union international, and had been an RAF pilot during the War, achieving the rank of wing commander.)

Another man in a senior position who had 'stood by his men' during the Hixon Inquiry was Wynns' most experienced director, H. P. 'Percy' Wynn, who said in his evidence that if he had been behind the wheel of the forward tractor, in the position that Bryn Groves was in, then he would have acted in exactly the same manner. Percy Wynn makes the point that he would not have had the opportunity to see the dual-purpose signboard, particularly if it was at the angle he had seen it at on the afternoon of 6 January, which was parallel to the carriageway.

Gibbens does mention in his penultimate Finding, number 12, that: 'The Ministry drafted the Emergency Notice in such a form that it was likely not to attract the attention of drivers who ought to have complied with the telephone procedure.' Which watered down the Ministry's responsibility for the putting in place of the pernicious signboard, about as far as it was possible to do.

In his final Finding (13), Gibbens states: 'The origin of the accident was in the failure of officers of both the Ministry and British Railways in collaboration to appreciate the measures necessary to deal with a hazard of which they were aware.' By bringing up this 'failure ... in collaboration' Gibbens merely touches upon what was the state of downright hostility, between the Inspectorate and the senior management of the Railways' S&T Department, which certainly worked against the Inspectorate even dimly appreciating the various lethal accident possibilities there were with AHB crossings, other than the one they obsessed over: impatient motorists being tempted to zigzag. On the other hand, as Gibbens was aware, the S&T Department had made the necessary adjustments to actual British Railways' working practices regarding 'exceptional or heavy loads' from 1964 onwards, by posting up detailed instructions in signal-boxes as to how signalmen should respond if phoned from an AHB crossing by the driver of a vehicle carrying such a load. These instructions complied with the dual-purpose signboard that the Ministry had instructed them to use. Again, the impression given is that Gibbens was seeking to spread responsibility away from the Ministry. (On the last day of the inquiry in his summing up for British Railways, their counsel, Edgar Fay, said that they now recognized that they should have been more stringent with the Ministry over the design of the dual-purpose signboard.)

Perhaps it is unfair to criticize Gibbens too much for his deliberations and findings as far as the Hixon disaster itself is concerned; he was working under extreme pressure after all to get the report out and implemented before any more AHB crossing accidents occurred. The inquiry transcripts and associated materials were well in excess of a million and a half words, so even with the assistance of Inquiry Secretary, Patrick Jackson, Gibbens carried out a Herculean task in just over a month. Having said this, and without too much speculation, it is possible to discern within the report and its findings a potential and very different apportionment of the culpability for the Hixon disaster, one in which virtually the full primary responsibility redounds onto the Wynns' forward tractor crew, who had 'failed to comply' with the signboard, which Gibbens had ruled was in a position to be read by approaching motorists. Note that failing to comply with a legal traffic sign is an offence under the criminal law; it doesn't matter whether the sign is seen or not, its mere presence means that road users are under an obligation to comply with its instructions. Colin Parsons in particular is singled out by Gibbens, having been clearly identified in paragraph 102, as not doing his job as a 'statutory attendant' according to its legal description, which was: ' "to give warning to the driver and to any other person of any danger likely to be caused ... by reason of the presence of the vehicle on the road". Under cross-examination on the subject of road signs, he said: "If I see a notice I would point it out to Mr Groves, but personally I do not think it is part of my duty." Consequently, he did not observe the emergency notice, as he should have done. He considered his job was to do as he was told by the leading driver.' This is a particularly stringent judgement on Parsons, stemming in part from Gibbens's misapprehension of what Parsons would have been doing as the forward tractor slowed to two mph to go over a level-crossing; from roughly thirty yards out Parsons would have been in front of the tractor, walking backwards and signalling to the driver as to his correct steering. Gibbens seems to have thought that Parsons was sitting in the passenger seat of the tractor, ignoring traffic signs! Gibbens states in paragraph 330 that he had concluded that the 'Emergency Notice' (the dual-purpose signboard) did not constitute a traffic sign under the British Transport Commission Act, 1957. If it had been regarded as a legal traffic sign, then Parsons could have found himself bearing the full responsibility for having disregarded it, and probably with the prospect of facing a Manslaughter charge for gross negligence.

(There is an intriguing and unusual opinion available to us as to Chairman Gibbens's abilities as a judge, in that one of this country's most highly regarded twentieth-century novelists, C. P. Snow, closely based a character in his 1974 novel with a legal background, *In Their Wisdom,* on Gibbens. 'Mr Justice Bosanquet' is described as being 'a shrewd and able man' but tending to rely too much on 'intuition'. Snow was not a friend of Gibbens, as such, but rather an acquaintance, who had the opportunity to observe him and converse with him, as a dinner companion at the London club of which they were both members.)

Having reviewed the events of 6 January 1968 at Hixon crossing as exhaustively investigated and adjudicated upon by Brian Gibbens, a brief description of what happened, focusing just on the actions of the four men, who had they acted differently on that day, could have prevented a collision, is perhaps worthwhile.

The time is around 12.20 p.m., the Wynns transporter with its 120-ton transformer load has just turned off the A51 onto Station Road, preceded by its escorting police car. Firstly, we have the police escort, PC Anthony Nicholls and PC Ephraim Prince; both men had started road traffic-related duties a few days beforehand and it is fair to say both were effectively totally naïve as to the operation of the new AHB crossings, both only ever having driven across open AHB crossings before, either on or off duty. What they saw, as their police car approached the crossing, was an open crossing; the barriers were raised and the way was clear. Their only possible point of existing reference to a closed level-crossing would have been with the old, fully gated variety where if the gates were shut, then it was impossible to proceed, but if they were open, then you could cross the railway. The two men had seen the road signs on the approach to the crossing, advising what to do if the lights were flashing and the bells were ringing: stop. What they had *not* seen was the one thing that might have saved the day, the 'IN EMERGENCY – PHONE SIGNALMAN' signboard. (Both policemen later that afternoon following the collision, and in evidence to the inquiry, said they had not seen it at all.) They drove across the lines and proceeded to the Hixon English Electric depot, the entrance to which was on the left-hand side, only a hundred or so yards away down the straight narrow lane. Once there, PC Nicholls got out of the car and pointed to the entrance. 'This is the place' was all that he intended to signal to the crew of the oncoming transporter, which although within clear sight, was still on the other side of the lines. Nicholls got back into the car and Prince turned it round in the entrance bay and proceeded back towards the crossing, where they pulled up to observe.

Bryn Groves, the driver of the forward tractor on Wynns' transporter, and his assistant in the forward tractor, Colin Parsons, were the third and fourth men whose actions could have avoided catastrophe had they been different; but as with the two escorting policemen they had no real prompt to act in any other way than that which brought about disaster. Let us look at the situation as it would have presented itself to Groves, as he sat, eight feet six inches above the carriageway in his driving seat on the left-hand side of his tractor, approaching the crossing along the narrow, but straight and level Station Road . He had cut his speed to 4 mph upon leaving the A51 roundabout . He saw that the crossing barriers were up, that the level-crossing was therefore open; in his experience, limited as it was to the familiar fully gated crossings, an open crossing did not suddenly become a closed crossing whilst a road vehicle was occupying it. What he did not see, or have drawn to his attention was the 'IN EMERGENCY – PHONE SIGNALMAN' signboard, with its inserted lower-case message of 'or before crossing with exceptional or heavy loads or cattle'. So therefore, he did not have the opportunity to ponder and decide whether his enormous vehicle qualified as 'exceptional or heavy' enough for him to phone the signalman. (Or more likely, as he would certainly have done many times before with one of the old manned crossings, *if it was closed to the road*, request that his police escort negotiate with the railway.) About fifty yards out from the crossing Groves slowed to two mph to enable the huge transporter to line up straight, to 'take' the crossing. Groves was not really concerned with the height of his vehicle and its enormous load, even though he was about to take it under 25-kilovolt electric wiring. This was for two reasons: firstly, he knew that the Railway invariably allowed an extra two feet of headroom when they specified sixteen feet six inches on the warning sign, to guard against the possibility of 'arcing' of current from the wires, so plenty of clearance available for his sixteen-feet-nine-inch-high load. Secondly, Groves knew that Wynns had taken five loads similar to his own, across Hixon crossing during the previous six months; in particular he knew that his fellow senior driver, Tommy Cromwell, had taken another Special Order load across, with an even larger and heavier transformer on board a month earlier on 7 December 1967. (What he didn't know was that Cromwell had asked his police escort to phone the signalman, not to see if it was safe to cross, but to check that his vehicle had enough height clearance. For Cromwell, finding out if he had height clearance, fortuitously provided the signalman on duty that day, with the opportunity to get him safely across the railway lines, which is what happened, more by luck than judgement, as we shall see in chapter 9.) A month later, Groves wasn't worried about the height clearance (correctly as it turned out, as it played no part in the ensuing catastrophe). Meanwhile, Colin Parsons, Groves' assistant, had dismounted from the forward tractor as it slowed to two mph, and then put himself twenty feet or so to the front, in line of sight of Groves and approached the level-crossing walking backwards, in the middle of the road. Whilst glancing behind him, he would have looked towards the oncoming behemoth to make sure it was lining up straight on to the crossing, and with a roughly equal amount of carriageway on either side of each front wheel arch. He would have been beckoning Groves on, or signalling any necessary adjustments with his hands, his attention would have been entirely on the spatial relationship between Wynns' sixteen-feet-nine-inch-wide vehicle and the available twenty-feet width of the carriageway over the crossing. He would not have had any opportunity to look around him for signboards, whilst he did his job.

As Parsons' heels shuffled onto the road decking of the crossing at around 12.24 p.m., the last chance to avert disaster disappeared. The 11.30 express from Manchester Piccadilly to Euston was two minutes away and travelling towards the crossing at approximately 85 mph. At 1,000 yards out from the crossing the express 'struck in' to the treadle, activating the mechanism: twenty-four seconds later it would be on the crossing. In those twenty-four seconds several things happened which to some extent prevented the disaster being any worse than it actually was. Firstly, when the bells began to ring and the red lights to flash Groves was already clear of the crossing in the forward tractor; looking to his left, and because of a curve on the line, he was able to see the express coming on at speed, about 800 yards away. Immediately, he accelerated, attempting to get as much of his load across as possible. In the rear tractor the driver, Mr Alan Illsley, saw the warning lights and heard the bells and in an act of calculated bravery and resolve, also accelerated; in order to get as much of the vast bulk of the transformer, which loomed in front of him, out of the way of the train. By doing this Illsley was bringing himself closer to the likely point of impact, and looking to his left he would have seen the express rounding the gentle curve about 400 yards away. The driver of the train, Mr Stanley Turner, had those same 400 yards in which to react, because that was his first sight of the blocked crossing. Taking into account reaction time and time for the mechanism to work, the train's brakes locked on at around 300 yards out, slowing it to around 75 mph at the point of impact. Illsley later recalled the terrible sight of Turner crouched over the controls, staring fixedly ahead of him. By their actions Groves, Illsley and Turner had produced a situation where the point of impact came on the weakest point of the transporter rig, the so called 'swan neck' connecting the low-loader platform to the rear bogie assembly. The locomotive cut through the transporter and careered onwards, causing the 120-ton transformer to turn through 90° and fly through the air for a distance of about twenty feet, so that it ended up to the outside of the Up line. If the impact had been onto the huge slab-like mass of the transformer itself, then the final death toll would unquestionably have been much higher.

Turner's body was the last to be recovered from the wreckage of his train, at 11.40 that night.

Some eight hours earlier, at around 3.45, British Railways Divisional Testing Assistant, Peter Owen, arrived at Hixon to carry out tests on the remaining, intact, AHB circuits and equipment. He noted that whilst the Upside 'Emergency Notice' signboard had been destroyed by the collision, the Downside signboard was 'clean, still facing the road, but leaning on the fence'.

Owen said this in evidence to the initial inquiry carried out by British Railways on Monday 8 January 1968. Also at this inquiry was S&T Inspector Francis Gubbins, who confirmed that on the Saturday afternoon he had seen the Downside signboard in the same position that Owen described. He also confirmed that the Ministry Inspecting Officer (Colonel Reed) had specified 'the turning of the notice from an angle of 45 degrees to parallel to the road'. He went on to explain that on the Upside, that notice had remained at 45 degrees to the carriageway, because it was too close to the crossing-keepers hut to alter.

This initial British Railways inquiry report was never made available to the Hixon Inquiry, although it was shared, immediately , with the Inspectorate. They didn't give it to the Hixon Inquiry either. The Inspectorate's copy is marked 'On no account to leave the office'.

Chapter 9

Tommy Cromwell: Tuesday, 5 December 1967

A miss is as good as a mile

Mr Groves's conduct was different from that of a fellow employee Mr T. W. Cromwell who drove a transformer from the Hixon airfield depot to the Pomona dock Manchester, on the 7th of December 1967: he telephoned to his employers' head office on the previous day for an assurance that the height of the wires was adequate, and, again, before venturing over the crossing on the day of his journey he asked the escorting police constable (P.c. Richards) to telephone to the signalman to ask whether he could safely pass under the wires.

Hixon Inquiry Report (paragraph 97)

Although Tommy Cromwell had successfully negotiated Hixon level-crossing with a Special Order vehicle and load on the morning of Thursday, 7 December 1967, that was not his first encounter with Hixon level-crossing. That had occurred two days earlier on the Tuesday afternoon and in four significant respects it was much more of an exact comparison with Bryn Groves' one and only experience. Firstly, Cromwell approached the crossing that Tuesday from the direction of the A51 (exactly as Groves did a month later). He was bringing a trailer in, to be used to transport a 160-ton transformer away from Hixon English Electric depot.

Secondly, Cromwell was driving a Special Order vehicle and even when it was 'empty', his transporter qualified as an 'SO' because of its extreme length alone: it was 168 feet long from the front of the forward tractor to the back of the rear 'pushing' tractor. This poses an interesting question: was Cromwell's vehicle under police escort? Certainly it would have been usual for an 'SO' to have had a police escort. In his witness statement Cromwell does not say, one way or the other.

Thirdly, following Wynns' usual procedure Cromwell would have slowed his enormous vehicle down to walking pace, in order to avoid damaging the level-crossing's wooden roadbed as he went over what was an open crossing: the barriers were up and there were no flashing lights or ringing bells. Therefore it would have taken his 168-feet-long vehicle over a minute to clear the crossing ... and as we know the time sequence for AHB operation was twenty-four seconds from 'striking-in' to the train arriving on the crossing; therefore if a train had triggered the crossing mechanism whilst his transporter was on it, Cromwell would have suffered the same fate as Groves did a month later. It was mere chance that he did not.

Finally, and most significantly of all, on this his first run across Hixon crossing, Cromwell saw no signboard warning of the need to telephone if driving 'an exceptional or heavy vehicle' as he approached the crossing from the direction of the A51. That is what he said in his witness statement; furthermore he asserts that he saw only the back of such a signboard on the opposite side of the road, as he glanced across curiously as he was driving slowly past it. He did not actually read the crucial message on the signboard until he returned to the crossing the following day (Wednesday 6th) from the direction of the airfield, this time just driving his uncoupled tractor, alone. The barriers were down and he stopped; the signboard was facing towards oncoming traffic, hence Cromwell read it, *remembered it and therefore* on Thursday 7th, requested his police escort, PC Richards, to phone the signalman, to make certain that there was enough clearance under the wires. Cromwell further states that he did not see the equivalent signboard in the same 'facing on-coming traffic' position, on the other side of the road; that signboard according to Cromwell was parallel to the carriageway. (Exactly as the S&T Inspector described the siting of the two signboards. See page 103.)

So, as can be seen, when faced with the same circumstances on Tuesday, 5 December, Cromwell's conduct was not different in any respect to that of Groves. He only acted differently *after* he had read the crucial notice, and that was not to check if it was safe to cross, but merely to check that the height clearance was adequate. Bryn Groves never had the chance to read the signboard as Cromwell did, and therefore in that respect the criticism of him in paragraph 97 is entirely spurious.

Turning, briefly, to what actually happened on the morning of 7 December 1967, it was in many ways a 'dry run' for the Hixon accident itself, although all concerned had luck with them that day. Unlike on 6 January, Cromwell's escort, PC Richards, did call the signalman to check out the height clearance, which allowed the signalman to tell him that it was safe to go under the wires. At this point Cromwell was proceeding in his laden 168-feet-long transporter towards what he thought was an open crossing, with his police escort on the other side of it. Fortuitously, Cromwell was going even more slowly than he would usually have done, because the road surface was icy and therefore the traction was bad. According to his witness statement, as he was closing in on the crossing, a train whizzed by in front of him, and, as he put it, he was only 'saved from disaster' by the icy road surface, otherwise he would already have been blocking the crossing when the train came. This was the maximum point of danger past; with the transporter stationary, another train ran over the crossing and then the signalman on duty in Colwich box, Mr H. W. Haldon was able to give them clearance to get the transporter across, safely, when PC Richards called him again.

At this distance in time, and given that Chairman Gibbens chose to misinterpret, or ignore, Cromwell's near-miss in order to criticize Groves, it seems pointless to draw any more conclusions from what happened on 7 December. Except to say, that it appears remarkable from the perspective of 2017, that all three men involved – Senior Driver Cromwell, Police Constable Richards and Signalman Haldon – did not report the occurrence at the time, to their various superiors; but then, the Health and Safety culture that would have demanded that they did so, was at least a couple of decades off, into the future. In 1967, it was still the case that 'a miss is as good as a mile'. (Haldon actually said in his witness statement referring to this incident, that signalmen were not required to report on any vehicles crossing the railway lines, so he didn't. Remember, this was the first and only time before the Hixon collision that anybody had phoned from the crossing, concerning whether it was safe to proceed or not. It was not until after the recommendations of the *Hixon Inquiry Report* that a 'crossing book' was introduced for each AHB, so that any incidents could be logged as a matter of course.)

Chapter 10

The dogs that didn't bark

The first and most important 'dog' was the Assistant General Manager of Western Region, Mr H. M. Lattimer and his non-appearance as a witness at the Inquiry; his 'famous' letter was a main focus of the Inquiry and he should have been asked to explain it personally and in detail. At this stage, nearly fifty years away from the proceedings, it is pointless to speculate as to why he wasn't called upon to give an account of himself, but it didn't look good at the time and it still doesn't.

Secondly, Mr Leslie Lloyd and Mr Brennan, the Movements Managers from Western Region, should also have been called upon to confront Colonel Reed personally with their assertion that he had been told about the Leominster incident of 8 November 1966, in February of 1967, ten months prior to the Hixon accident; again, it didn't look good at the time and it still doesn't.

Thirdly, 'the keen young amateur photographer, Mr Iain Campbell' never appeared before the inquiry, to state, and face cross-examination, as to when exactly he took the two crucial photographs of Hixon crossing. Given that the photographs were used to determine 'with some certainty' the position of the 'Emergency Notice' signboard on 6 January 1968, it would have been interesting, to say the least, to have had more detail about their provenance.

The fourth and final 'dog' is why the Inspectorate were never asked to explain why they had changed the policy at AHB crossings, to one of having no telephones for the use of the public as the standard installation model from 1963 onwards. An explanation might have led to Chairman Gibbens beginning to understand that the Inspectorate were not the disinterested implementers of policy that he assumed them to be. Gibbens never really 'got' how much the Inspectorate ruled the roost on Britain's railways prior to Hixon. This was not the case after Hixon; both Colonel Reed and Colonel McMullen left the Inspectorate in 1968, before their time. Mr Scott-Malden, not surprisingly, carried on a serene progress up the Civil Service ladder, becoming a deputy secretary at the Ministry, although Richard Marsh sacked the Permanent Secretary, Sir Thomas Padmore, in July 1968, a year before he was due to retire, which was considered quite revolutionary at the time. A year earlier, of course, Marsh had been the Minister of Power, who had, eventually, brought the Chairman of the National Coal Board, Lord Robens, to admit that the Aberfan disaster had been a result of the Board's policy decisions. Also, Marsh had started his parliamentary career in 1960, by initiating what is generally regarded as the precursor of modern Health and Safety legislation: The Offices, Shops and Railway Premises Act, 1961. In the light of these facts, it does not seem entirely fanciful to suggest that the PM, Harold Wilson, put Marsh in place at Transport in the middle of the AHB crisis, as a technocratic 'new broom' to sort out a situation where the Railways Group / Railway Inspectorate had overstepped the mark as far as the running of the railways was concerned, with disastrous results, literally. British Railways certainly welcomed Marsh a couple of years later as its effective and dynamic chairman for five years from 1971to 1976. Marsh, in his autobiography, *Off the Rails*, states that in his experience the British Civil Service 'made the Mafia look amateurish' in terms of their ruthlessness and propensity for in-fighting; certainly the hostility between the Inspectorate and the S&T Department of British Railways described in this book leads one to think that Marsh had a point. Also, there was the clear, and highly dangerous, squabbling over the positioning of the 'IN EMERGENCY' signboard, between Colonel Reed and Mr Alexander of the Roads Engineering Division; twenty-five years previously they would have been fighting the Germans and Japanese, but by the mid-1960s they were fighting each other.

For the Hixon Inquiry, the painstakingly adversarial legal process itself, certainly mitigated against producing anything other than the 'rockets all round' result that *Commercial Motor* identified in its 2 August 1968 edition: If Everybody is to blame, then Nobody is to blame. However, others were not convinced that the culpability for the Hixon disaster should have been shared out so equitably. Mrs Barbara Blake the widow of Mr Keith Blake and mother of Jill Blake, aged ten, both killed at Hixon, would have read the report when it came out. She had also sat through the many days of hearings, and observed the seven Ministry witnesses grinding their way to the finish, 'the machine' as the newspaper reports called them. Mrs Blake initiated a private prosecution against those whose negligence she believed contributed to the disaster, her order of Defendants put the Ministry of Transport first, followed by British Railways, with Wynns third and the Staffordshire Police in fourth place. Judging from what has been revealed in this book, it seems that Mrs Blake was much closer to the truth of things than Chairman Gibbens.

As to the 'truth' about whether AHB crossings were safe enough, as they had been installed up until the Hixon disaster, there exists an editorial from the *Railway Gazette* of 3 May 1968; Colonel McMullen, then still the Inspectorate's Chief Inspecting Officer, thought so highly of this piece, entitled 'Hard facts on half-barriers', that he had a copy sent to Brigadier Gardiner, one of the assessors for the Hixon Inquiry. It is reproduced as plate 24 and as can be seen, claims that the Hixon disaster was a freak accident and argues robustly for the status quo to be maintained. Having read a number of documents written by Colonel Reed, the author of this book considers that 'Hard facts on half-barriers' probably came from Colonel Reed; certainly it reflects the opinions he espoused vigorously throughout the Hixon Inquiry and shows that he still considered 'his' AHB crossings to be perfectly safe.

Robert Wynn and Sons Ltd do not seem to have been unduly affected by the unwelcome notoriety that the Hixon disaster brought upon them, at least not in terms of their day-to-day operations. H. P. Wynn, the senior director who had stood squarely beside his firm's employees during the Hixon Inquiry, went on to receive an OBE a couple of years later for 'services to the Road Haulage Industry'. On a somewhat macabre note, Wynns head office in Newport used to get an empty, black-bordered envelope through the post, on the anniversary of the collision, for at least ten years afterwards. It was addressed simply to 'The Directors'.

Generally, the one thing that is surprising from the perspective of 2017 is how quickly we have forgotten just how important the Second World War was in shaping the nature of modern Britain in very direct ways, well into the 1960s and probably beyond. In particular, the fact that not only the entire Railway Inspectorate, but many if not most, of the senior management of British Railways had been officers in the Royal Engineers, now seems quite remarkable in our largely demilitarized society.

Precursor: Leominster, Kington junction level-crossing, 4 May 1965

Given that my father did make his crucial phone call at Leominster, using a handset positioned permanently on the Ludlow side of the crossing, for the use of farmers seeking to bring livestock over it, how did this phone come to be placed there? The answer to this question is to be found in the Ministry of Transport Initial Site Inspection report of 4 May 1965; this document also shows that the Railway Inspectorate were willing to mendaciously deny the existence of a telephone of any type at Leominster crossing. Because by doing so they were able to say that it was one of the last crossings to come into operation before the September 1966 decision of British Railways, requiring public access telephones at all automatic crossings, came into force, and thereby conceal the truth of Colonel Reed's antipathy to phones. The very last thing the Inspectorate wanted was a detailed examination, in open court, of the hair-raisingly incompetent process by which the Leominster crossing had been converted to automatic working. These Ministry of Transport Initial Site Inspections, were, as Chairman Gibbens acerbically noted, 'for the convenience of the Railway'. In short, if it had been decided by the Railway Inspectorate and British Railways, that a particular crossing was suitable for automation then the views of the local community, as to particular local circumstances, were to be listened to, but not necessarily given much, if any, weight when it came to deciding whether to press on with the automation, or indeed whether any specific alterations needed to be made to the 'standard' conversion in order to take account of such local circumstances.

According to the minutes of the Site Inspection, presenting the case for the automation of Leominster, Kington Junction crossing on 4 May 1965, was Colonel Reed of the Railway Inspectorate, assisted by Major Olver. Amongst those in attendance representing various legitimate interests, was Mr W. Sparey, on behalf of the National Farmers' Union. Colonel Reed, as far as we can judge from the minutes, and the separate Detailed Specification Order, nearly achieved an almost complete victory, in that an unmodified level-crossing was to be installed, without public access telephones, or indeed permanent telephones of any kind. Whether Colonel Reed gave his full-blown site meeting speech we don't know; the model text of this, of which there is a copy, is dated November 1965 and takes approximately twenty minutes to deliver.

Although he may not have said so on this occasion, Colonel Reed is on record as stating that he did not see the point of 'emergency' telephones, because they would be of no use if a vehicle was stuck on a crossing once the barriers had descended, and anyway such telephones might be subject to misuse or vandalism by local youths.

Mr W. Sparey made the point that, given the crossing's semi-rural location with open fields close by on both sides of the railway, cattle grids were a necessity and that in addition a telephone on the Ludlow (countryside) side of the crossing should be provided so that livestock could be safely walked from fields on one side of the crossing to fields on the other. Fairly uncontroversial and sensible requests one would have thought, which accurately reflected local conditions, but Colonel Reed didn't take kindly to them at all, and, according to the minutes, 'would not accept that on a highway of this nature there was need to take into account the movement of cattle over the crossing'. However, Reed's views were ignored, because the minutes go on to state: 'the request of the National Farmers' Union for cattle grids to be provided at the crossing *and also a telephone* [my italics] would be met'. Presumably, British Railways provided the secretarial support for the minute-taking and it was, after all, their crossing. So despite Reed's general opposition to full public access emergency telephones integral to the barriers, and in this case even a single post phone for farmers, British Railways was able to sneak one in, within the terms of the 1963 Requirements.

That, therefore, is how there happened to be a telephone in place at Leominster crossing: as an afterthought, its installation actively opposed by the man with overall responsibility for the safe working of the crossing. At the Hixon Inquiry on 7 March 1968 the Railway Inspectorate chose to deny the existence of any telephone for the use of the public at all at the crossing. Although Colonel Reed would have become aware that British Railways had provided a telephone for use by farmers against his wishes, but not until he had carried out his hasty reassessment of the situation at Leominster, on 8 March 1968. Not surprisingly, he didn't point this inconvenient fact out in the three short Leominster documents he produced for the Hixon Inquiry. As it turned out, Reed having to go to the trouble of producing these documents was a waste of his time, because the Inquiry had moved on to other matters. Good.

Mr W. 'Bill' Sparey, the NFU representative at the May 1965 Site Inspection, farmed land, through which until September 1964, just a few months previously, part of the Leominster to Kington branch line had run. He was therefore well used to interacting with the railway on a daily basis and would have been keen to ensure that the new crossing had a phone which enabled people to communicate with the railway, should they need to do so. For Colonel Reed, on the other hand, the overriding concern, apparently to the exclusion of *all other considerations*, was that trains should always approach the crossing at their maximum operating speed. In other words, the crossing, instead of being integrated into its semi-rural situation, was to be isolated, as though the railway was a closed, perfect system.

Postscript

lthough the events I have described from 1966 and 1968, happened only around fifty years ago, they do seem to belong to a far more distant age, where deference to those in positions of authority in particular, appeared to be an ingrained part of the national character …

Sir Clive Bossom, Conservative MP for North Herefordshire, came canvassing during the 1970 General Election, down our street of 'Homes fit for Heroes' council houses, with their extensive gardens, both front and rear. My dad was outside mowing the lawn, and placed squarely in a flowerbed facing the road was a 'Vote Labour' signboard. The eleven-year-old me was in the garden too, and I observed Sir Clive pause to consult his polling sheet, and then make a bee line for our front gate! He obviously hadn't seen the signboard and I was sure that my socialist dad would give him short-shrift. However, to my surprise, the two men soon became engaged in what seemed to be an extremely amicable conversation, with my dad doing most of the talking. I moved a little closer to try to overhear what they were saying, at which point my dad told me to go and fetch him a glass of water. I ran off quickly, hoping to be able to get back in time to find out what they had been talking about, and why Sir Clive seemed to be the one who was doing all the listening. However, all I saw when I returned was the two men shaking hands, with the MP gazing at my dad with a look that puzzled me at the time, but which I now realize was one of admiration. Then he was gone. That memory lay buried in my subconscious for over forty years, until I came across copies of letters from Sir Clive in the Hixon files at the National Archive, together with references to questions he had tabled in the House of Commons concerning the Leominster level-crossing. He, for one, certainly knew the true story of what had happened on the 8th of November, 1966.

Acknowledgements and Sources

It would have been very difficult to write this book without the input of a number of railwaymen, in particular my father's friend and colleague, Phil Jones, who helped flesh out the bones of the original story and provided some probably, now, unique technical information about the process of AHB crossing installation during the 1960s, as well as a number of the photographs used in the book. Another contemporary of my father, Doug Jukes, now sadly deceased, was invaluable as far as his knowledge of correct railway procedure in the 1960s was concerned. Peter Goody provided an essential sounding board as the narrative gradually took shape and became more complex. Mike Kneen, locomotive driver – and incidentally Rector of Leominster – helped out in this respect too. Also Crew Commander Brian Rodgers.

I exchanged a number of cordial and useful emails with the noted railway historian, Adrian Vaughan, so thanks are due to him.

In complement to the Railway side of things, having access to the Wynn family's archive gave the book its other necessary dimension; in particular, allowing me the use of photographs which had literally been undeveloped and unseen for nearly fifty years, gives the story of the Hixon collision an immediacy that it would otherwise lack. I was also able to pick the brains of John Wynn and his son Peter, as to the working practices of heavy haulage crews that were in place at the time. (Also Peter's daughter Daisy, who fielded my initial phone call, and said 'Wow, that sounds like something Grandad would be interested in!')

Peter Wynn gave me an interesting anecdote concerning Arthur Rees, the Chief Constable of Staffordshire: he was introduced to Rees, who was at the time (early 1980s) President of Eccleshall rugby club. On discovering that Peter was a member of the Wynn family, the Hixon collision came up and Rees said that when he got to the scene of the accident, he had immediately recognized Bryn Groves because they had played club rugby together in South Wales. 'Hello Bryn,' he had said, 'what on earth has happened here?' To which came the dazed reply, 'Hello Arthur. We were going across the lines and a train came along and hit us.' (This story led me to discover a rugby-related link of my own, in that my father's cousin, Glyn Prosser, also played alongside Arthur Rees, but this time in the 1935 Welsh XV that beat the mighty All Blacks 13-12.)

In terms of practical help relating to the book I would like to mention David Till of D-Technics, Clevedon, for quickly sorting out any computer glitches that came up. Also the staff of That Copy Shop, Clevedon, for making sure I was able to capture the quality of images I required.

Thanks must go of course to John Scott-Morgan, Janet Brookes and their colleagues at Pen and Sword for giving me the opportunity to write this book, and to Chris Cocks, my editor.

Last but certainly not least, my heartfelt thanks go to my wife, Linda, for her love and support during the five years it has taken to produce this book.

Archival Sources

Extensive use has been made of the records kept at the National Archives, Kew; mainly the Hixon Inquiry transcripts, but also the more general Ministry of Transport files, relating to the installation of Automatic Half-Barrier crossings from the 1950s through to the 1980s. Special thanks are due to the staff at Kew, who were unfailingly helpful and courteous.

Acknowledgement must also go to the head office staff of the Associated Society of Locomotive Engineers and Firemen, for letting me rummage through their collection of Proceedings and Journals.

(I would like to mention the Open University (founded 1969) but can only do so in a roundabout way ... When I was tracking down a hard copy of the *Hixon Inquiry Report* a bookseller told me of a series of television programmes put out by the OU in the early 1970s, entitled something like 'Bringing about Change: People and Systems' that featured the introduction of AHB level-crossings into Britain as a prime example of how *not* to bring about change. Intrigued, I contacted the OU archive, but whilst confirming that they *had* put out such programmes in the early 1970s, they had no copies of them or any accompanying written materials, because in the early days they didn't keep any stuff once it had gone out! So somewhere, in somebody's attic or garage, there may be lurking video tapes of men wearing stripy tank tops and sporting Zapata moustaches, telling the whole sorry AHB story.)

Newspapers

I was fortunate to have at my disposal a large press cuttings album compiled by Wynns' office staff at the time, but consisting of every newspaper article referencing the Hixon disaster and inquiry, supplied to them by the International Press-cutting Bureau for the period 7 January 1968 to 31 May 1968. (As far as individual titles are concerned I have referenced each quotation within the text, and they include all the national titles we are still familiar with today: *The Times, Telegraph, Guardian, Mail, Mirror* etc., together with a strong showing from regional titles such as the *South Wales Argus* and the *Birmingham Post* that had a huge readership back in the 1960s. The newspaper reports were key to enabling me to reflect what the public were being told about the AHB crossings, and how they were reacting.)

Books

Highway Code, 1959 edition (revised 1961) (Her Majesty's Stationery Office, 1961)

Report of the Public Inquiry into the Accident at Hixon Level Crossing on January 6th, 1968
(Her Majesty's Stationery Office, July, 1968)

Bradley, Simon: *The Railways Nation Network and People* (Profile Books Ltd, 2015)

Hall, Stanley and Van Der Mark, Peter: *Level Crossings* (Ian Allen Publishing, 2008)

Hall, Stanley: *Railway Detectives* (Ian Allen Publishing, 1990)

Jones, Robin: *Beeching: The Inside Track* (Morton's Media Group Ltd, 2012)

Marsh, Richard: *Off the Rails* (Weidenfeld and Nicolson, 1978)

Orwell, George: *Collected Essays, Journalism and Letters Volume 1* (Secker & Warburg, 1968)

Richards, Jack and Searle, Adrian: *The Quintishill Conspiracy* (Pen and Sword, 2013)

Snow, C. P.: *In Their Wisdom* (Macmillan, 1974)

Vaughan, Adrian: *Obstruction Danger* (Patrick Stephens Ltd, 1989)

Wood, Gordon: *Railways of Hereford* (Gordon Wood, 2003)

DVDs

B&R Video Productions, Volume 99 of the Ultimate Archive Steam series *Herefordshire Byways*.

Online and broadcast sources

The Brighton branch of ASLEF web site for the report on the Roundstone Level-crossing Accident, that occurred on 25 September 1965, by Colonel W.P. Reed of Her Majesty's Railway Inspectorate.

BBC Radio 4, for a programme in the *Writing the Century* series, broadcast in 2016, which included a reference to the early Beeching plan, and its intention to close all the railway stations on the mainline between Holyhead and Chester.

BBC Television, for the two documentaries broadcast in October 2016 on the subject of the Aberfan disaster.

British Newspaper Archive

Commercial Motor Archive

railwaysarchive.co.uk – particularly for the report by Colonel J. R. H. Robertson of Her Majesty's Railway Inspectorate, on the level-crossing accident at Trent Road, Beckingham, Lincolnshire that occurred on Tuesday, 16 April 1968.

Wikipedia

YouTube – for the British Movietone News collection.

Index

A. E. Wyeth & Co. solicitors 64, 65
Aberfan
  Disaster 14, 107
  Tribunal 20, 67, 96
Acts
  British Transport Commission (1957)
    39, 100
  Offices, Shops and Railway Premises
    (1961) 108
  Regulation of Railways (1871) 22
AHB (Automatic Half Barrier) crossings 5, 7,
  10–12, 14–20, 22–27, 31–37, 39–41, 44, 45,
  49, 51, 53–55, 57–61, 64, 67, 69–87, 90–92,
  96–100, 105–109
Alexander, F. S. 12, 58, 72, 80, 91, 108
AOCR (Automatic Open Crossings) 59
Associated Society of Locomotive Engineers
  and Firemen 24
Automatic Half Barrier crossings *see* AHB
Automatic Open Crossings *see* AOCR

Banwell, Mr 43
Beeching, Dr Richard x, 7, 10
Berry, Grenville 15, 91
Bickerton, F. D. 23, 34, 35, 37, 40
Birmingham Post 60–62, 66, 94
Blake, Barbara 108
Blake, Jill 108
Blake, Keith 108
Blennerhassett, Mr 82
Blower, Austen 47, 49, 50, 52, 60, 75, 76
Board of Trade 28
Bossom, Sir Clive MP 57, 112
Brennan, Mr 55, 73, 74, 81–83
Bridge, Nigel QC 23
British Movietone News 40
British Railways 1, 2, 5–7, 9, 10, 12, 13,
  24–26, 27, 32, 33, 35, 37, 39, 40, 42–45, 47,
  49, 52–55, 57, -60, 62, 65, 67, 71–75, 77–82,
  88, 90–93, 97, 99, 108–111
  Board 7, 26, 33, 47, 78

Regions
  Eastern 1, 6, 45
  London Midland 6
  North Eastern 6
  Scotland 6
  Southern 6, 86, 90
  Western 6, 26, 32, 42, 45, 47, 60–62, 68,
    73–75, 78–81, 107
  S&T Department 12, 45, 71, 77–80, 82, 86,
    99, 108
British Transport Commission 1
Brown, George MP 16
Buchanan, Prof Colin 15, 33, 36, 37, 82, 86,
  90, 92

Campbell, Iain 93, 107
Cardiff x, 55, 56, 74
Castle, Barbara MP 10, 14, 20, 21, 24,
  57, 64, 87
Cockburn, Mr 25, 26
Colliery Officials and Staffs Association
  see also Aberfan Disaster Tribunal 20
'Colonel Gower' incident *see also* Gower,
  Lt-Col 6, 45, 59–61, 74
Commercial Motor xii, 108
Conservative Government 10
Court Lees Approved School, Inquiry into
  14, 20
Cromwell, T. C. 'Tommy' 5, 102, 104–106

Daily Mail 57
Derby Evening Telegraph 16
Dutch Ministry of Transport *see* Rijksdienst
  voor het wegerkeer

English Electric Co. Ltd 25, 84, 97, 101, 104

Fay, Edgar 24, 82, 99
Finer, Morris 70

Gardiner, Brig Richard 15, 108
Gaylor, Asst Chief Constable 57

General Election (1964) 16
General Election (1970) 112
Gibbens. E. Brian QC 13–15, 19–22, 24, 25, 35, 37, 43–45, 47, 49, 56, 60, 61, 65, 67–71, 75, 80, 81, 83, 84, 87, 89–100, 106–108, 110
Gilmour, M. H. B. 26, 27, 71
Gower, Lt-Col see also 'Colonel Gower' incident 50, 59–62
'Colonel Gower' incident see also Gower, Lt-Col 6, 45, 59–61, 74
Gower, Mrs 59–62
Graham, Mr 75
Groves, Bryn 30, 63, 94, 95, 97, 98, 100–106
Gubbins, Francis 103

Haldon, H. W. 106
Hale, F. M. 12, 91
Hallett, S&T inspector 9, 47–51, 53, 54, 78
Health and Safety 106, 108
Hereford 7, 8, 50, 54, 74
Hereford Times 60
Herefordshire Byways 51
Herefordshire County Council 57
Highway Code 38–40, 96
Hill, Alan 66, 94
Hilton, John 88, 89
Hixon see also level-crossings, Hixon AHB
    Hixon Inquiry x-xii, 6, 12–27, 30, 31, 33–35, 37, 38, 43–45, 47, 53, 54, 56–60, 63–66, 68,   73-   80, 82–85, 87, 89, 90–98, 107–109, 111
    Hixon Inquiry Report xii, 11–13, 17–19, 22–24, 30, 39, 41, 43, 44, 57, 67, 72, 81, 82, 84,   86,   97, 104, 106
Holland, A. D. 23, 24
Hopkins, Ronald 24
Horton, James 30, 41, 42, 44, 45, 47, 48, 50, 53, 67–70, 77

Ibbotson, Mr 75, 76, 80
Illsley, Alan 63, 102, 103
Imperial College (London) 15, 33

Jenkins, Roy MP 14, 20
John, Leslie 68
Jones, Arthur 47, 49
Jones, Peter 56
Jones, Phil 47, 49, 51, 54, 86
Jukes, Douglas 54

Kington ix

Labour Government 7, 10
Langley, Brig C. A. 85
Lattimer, H. M. 6, 31, 42–46, 55, 60, 61, 62, 67, 74, 76, 96, 107
Leominster incident see level-crossings, Leominster, Kington junction
level-crossings
    Birkdale (Southport) 80
    Bromfield (Ludlow), lack of track section signals at 51
    Hixon AHB ix, x, xii, 4, 5, 9, 10, 12–14, 16, 19–25, 28, 30, 37, 43, 52, 57, 59, 63–66, 72, 73, 76, 80–84, 87, 93–97, 100, 102, 104, 105, 107
    Leominster, Kington junction ix-xi, 5–8, 12, 15, 21, 26, 30, 41–62, 67–74, 77, 78, 80–82, 86, 87, 91, 96, 107, 110–112
    Lockington, accident at 59
    Pontsarn (Merthyr Tydfil) 80, 96
    Roundstone (Angmering), accident at 17
    Trent Road (Beckingham), accident at x, 85–89
    Yapton AHB, incident at 86, 88
Lloyd, Leslie 26, 47–49, 59, 68, 69, 71, 73, 78, 82, 83, 107
Lockington level-crossing accident see level-crossings, Lockington
locomotives 7, 8, 9, 30, 50–52, 60, 63, 92, 95, 103
    Class 37 Diesel 7, 8, 50
    Class 47 Diesel 52
Ludlow 5, 8, 48, 49, 51, 110, 111

Mackmurdie, Robert 64, 67, 93, 94
Madge, J. R. 23
Marples, Ernest MP 25
Marsh, Richard MP 88, 90, 91, 107, 108
McMullen, Col Denis xi, 6, 7, 10, 14, 23, 26, 34, 37, 41, 61, 62, 71, 74, 79, 83–86, 107, 108
McNaughton Lt-Col I. K. A. 10
Ministry of Transport xi, xii, 1, 6, 11, 12, 15–17, 19–23, 25, 26, 28, 30, 34, 35, 38, 39, 43, 45, 47, 57–61, 64, 65, 67–72, 74, 77–80, 82, 83, 87, 93, 96–98, 108, 110
    Railways Group see also Railway Inspectorate xi, 1, 6, 11, 37, 78, 91
    Road Engineering Division 2, 11, 57, 58, 91

Road Signs Division 91
  Traffic Engineering Division 83
Moreau, F/Lt R. D. 24, 93
Morning Star 20

National Archive (Kew) 47, 77, 112
National Coal Board *see also* Aberfan disaster
  and Tribunal 67, 96, 107
National Farmers' Union (NFU) 2, 69, 110
National Union of Mineworkers (NUM) *see
  also* Aberfan disaster *and* Tribunal 14, 20
Netherlands State Railways 17–19, 34, 37
Newport 7, 13, 63, 96, 109
Nicholls, PC Anthony 94, 97, 98, 100, 101

Off the Rails see Marsh, Richard MP
Olver, Maj Peter 10, 11, 23, 84, 110
Owen, Peter 103

Padmore, Sir Thomas 107
Parsons, Colin 94, 95, 100–102
Patrick Jackson, W. 21, 25, 87, 90, 99
Pemberton, Bert ix
Pickfords 83, 84
police 2, 5, 25, 35, 42, 57, 65, 83, 92, 94–96,
  100–102, 104–106, 108
  Staffordshire 25, 65, 79, 97
  West Mercia 57
Pomona Dock, Manchester 104
Presteigne ix
Preston, Mr 97
Prince, PC Ephraim 94, 97, 98, 100, 101

rail lines
  Brighton to Portsmouth 17
  Cardiff to Crewe 56
  Cardiff to Holyhead x
  Leominster to Kington ix, 111
  Manchester Piccadilly to Euston 9, 102
  Shrewsbury to Hereford *see also* Welsh
    Marches 7
  Welsh Marches x, 7, 55, 80, 87
  West Coast Main Line
    (Euston to Glasgow) 9, 10
Railway Gazette 108
Railway Inspectorate x–xii, 1, 2, 6, 10–15,
  17–19, 21–23, 25, 26, 29, 30, 32–34, 36,
  37, 39–41, 45, 49, 53, 56–63, 68, 71,
  72, 74–81, 84, 86, 87, 89, 91, 95, 99,
  107–111

railway stations
  Chester 7, 9, 10
  Euston 9, 102
  Glasgow 9
  Hereford 7, 8, 56, 74
  Holyhead 7
  Leominster x, 6, 8, 42, 50–52, 54, 58, 74
  Manchester Piccadilly 102
  Marylebone 40, 41
  Newport 7
  Shrewsbury 7
Read, Mr 68, 69, 78
Reading 9, 77, 78
Reed, Col W. P. x, 1–7, 10–12, 14, 17–20, 23,
  25, 26, 32, 34–38, 40, 41, 45, 47, 49, 55, 56,
  58, 61, 62, 68, 69, 71–86, 91, 92, 103, 107,
  108, 110, 111
Rees, Chief Constable Arthur
  65, 66, 94, 97, 98
Register, Brian 64, 65
Richards, PC 104–106
Rijksdienst voor het wegerkeer (Dutch
  Ministry of Transport) 19
road haulage 13, 96, 109
  Road Haulage Association (RHA) 27, 39
roads
  A49 7, 12
  A51 92, 100, 101, 104, 105
  Station 100
Robens, Lord 107
Robert Wynn & Sons Ltd *see* Wynns
Robertson, Col J. R. H. 10, 87–89
Roundstone accident *see* level-crossings,
  Roundstone (Angmering)
Rose, Cliff 58
Royal Commission 1966 (Lord Justice
  Salmon) 22

Salop 56
Scott-Malden, C. P. xi, 6, 7, 14, 15, 21, 23–25,
  34, 37, 61, 62, 74, 81, 83, 84, 107
signage 11, 12, 15, 67, 72, 90, 91, 96
Sparey, W. 'Bill' 110, 111
Stafford 56, 64
Stoke-on-Trent 64
Stott, Prof P. F. 59
Stuart, R. J. 56, 57, 87
Sunday Mail 94
Sunday Mercury 65
Sunday Mirror 93

T. A. Matthews solicitors 80
Tay Bridge Disaster 10, 22, 64
Taylor, P. L. 97, 98
The Daily Sketch 65
The Journal (Newcastle upon Tyne) 24
The Times 59, 67, 88
Thirty seconds, or Eternity 34, 35
Thompson, Noel 66, 94
Townsend-Rose, Lt-Col A. G. 59
Transport Commission *see* British Transport Commission
Treasury Solicitor's Department 23, 25, 26
Trent Road accident *see* level-crossings, Trent Road (Beckingham)
Turner, Stanley 103
Tyler, John 5, 77–79, 86, 91

Westwood, Jack 1, 7, 47
Williams, 'Flash' 51
Williams, Eddie 51
Wilson, Harold PM 87, 88, 108
Wynn, Gordon 63, 64
Wynn, H. P. (Percy) 63–65, 98, 109
Wynn, John 63, 64
Wynn, Noel 63, 64, 70
Wynns 5, 13, 15, 25, 32, 41–46, 53, 57, 60, 61, 63, 65–71, 74, 79, 81–84, 94–96, 98, 100–102, 104, 108, 109

Yapton accident *see* level-crossings, Yapton AHB